STRENGTH FOR THE SOUL

Strength for the Soul

Wisdom from Past and Present

Selected and arranged by

DOROTHY MASON FULLER

FORTRESS PRESS Philadelphia

Library of Congress Catalog Card Number 75–13037

ISBN 0–8006–0417–2

4969F75 Printed in U.S.A. 1–417

To C. P. F.,
dear comrade tramping mountain trails,
on travels to far lands and strange,
and this blest journey of discovery.
D. M. F.

CONTENTS

PREFACE

This book is a collection of wisdom of different eras, cultures, and faiths, chosen and arranged to bring comfort and strength to the distressed: to those who are confused or alarmed in this time of distorted values, crumbling standards, and dismaying violence; to those who are beset by suffering they cannot escape or problems they find insoluble alone; to those afflicted with health problems or terminal illness, and all who dread the thought of death.

Part 1, "The Need for Change," focuses on the failure of science and technology to meet basic human needs, on materialistic goals that have produced harmful stress, and then proposes a way of achieving a healthful balance in life.

Part 2, "The Challenge to Grow," focuses on suffering—its threat, its opportunity, its benefits—and ends with examples of those who triumphed spiritually over their ordeal.

Part 3, "Approaching the Unknown," focuses on preparation for the end of this life, and explores the need to revise values and goals to keep life meaningful under adverse conditions. It seeks to dispel fear and impart strength to approach what lies beyond the horizon.

THE NEED FOR CHANGE

Would man but wake from out his
  haunted sleep,
Earth might be fair, and all men glad
  and wise.

—Clifford Bax

"ONCE UPON A TIME . . ."

Once upon a time I needed desperately what these pages offer. I have prepared them for myself and for others, because consciously or unconsciously every human being is making the same journey of discovery. Some go joyously through the adventure of life, some with unrelenting fear of lurking dangers. By way of inward growth we travel, each at a different pace, toward the enlightenment that beckons just beyond the horizon.

All of us came out of darkness into a world totally strange and often disturbing. Childhood joys alternated with anguish. Some experiences maimed us; some left indelible scars on mind and heart.

In youth we began to probe for the meaning of the mystery, to wonder who we were and seek direction for our future. Alluring vistas beckoned in adolescence. How could we choose?

In youth there are always strong emotional drives to abolish massive corruption and injustice. Poetic visions of a "brave new world" mingle with powerful urges to create something of immortal worth—a world of peace and love and joy.

The lack of means to bring about needed change,

however, often means galling frustration. Youth cannot wait. It must be now. *They scorn traditional values. They abhor the sickness of our world, yet are blind to their own need for the wisdom to effect healing.*

Wisdom requires long apprenticeship. Intellect is the modern God: scientific method, they say, will solve all problems, supply all lacks; our jet age technology has outmoded man's need of divine guidance.

There are many of us who disagree. Prolonged search for a firm foundation to meet personal sorrows and trials has led us to opposite conclusions.

Not till a period of weakness and ill-health threatened my whole future did I consciously and earnestly set forth on my own journey toward the light. Parental veto had locked the door against a stage career. I expected marriage and motherhood to erase that disappointment. It did. To others' eyes I seemed to have no problems, and the future was full of promise. Inwardly, though, I was beset with fears.

There was never enough energy to accomplish what I saw to be done. Tensions I could not fathom made nights sleepless. Something was very wrong, I sensed; I must have help. Yet the trouble, I felt intuitively, was not physical. I started reading the Psalms. I tried prayer. I asked for guidance.

I was led to writings of wise men who have influenced men's thinking down the ages. I began to collect passages that nourished and strengthened me. At some point I suddenly understood that the imbalance I had sensed was due to a starved spirit. As I fed it daily, I grew strong.

By degrees, as faith increased, fears lessened and insomnia took its leave.

Prayer was indispensable to my well-being, I discovered—not just pleas for healing but for guidance, and thanksgiving for blessings I'd scarcely noted before. Living in two worlds at once set my life in balance, so long as I put spiritual concerns first. Unmistakable answers to prayer convinced me that an invisible, wise Creator of the Universe was also close to his human children in trouble and heard their cry for help. In that hard training period I learned the everlasting truth that we "cannot live by bread alone."

"Seek and ye shall find, knock and it shall be opened to you" are no mere biblical phrases. I have tested them over and over and my experience confirms them to be true. When in a crisis, utterly helpless, I found the courage to say "Let your will for me be done," that mysterious Presence who would direct every life for good if permitted, led me eventually into a useful and deeply satisfying life, "strong in the Lord."

Why do I make this personal witness? I had not intended to. People more important and better known than I would speak the truth for me out of their experience. But now, in these days of trouble, when our world and many lives within it are in deep turmoil and sinister forces seem bent on universal destruction, I feel it important to share with you the fact that in one of God's children acknowledgment of the anguished "need for change" resulted eventually in a purposeful, integrated life set free from fear. The sickness of our time and culture is surely critical but the outcome need not be fatal. Healing and strength depend on your response and mine to this great spiritual challenge.

Dorothy Mason Fuller

Change has always been unsettling to human beings and today we are experiencing a rate and scope of change men have never known. Another cause of our current unrest stems both directly and indirectly from the new knowledge and power that science and technology have given us. Such knowledge and power impose tremendous new responsibilities on man. And they are responsibilities from which we cannot turn because they involve his deepest relationships with nature, his man-made environment and his fellowman. . . . They are forcing us to do more than pay lip service to those things we have said we believed in—such as the brotherhood of man, the dignity of the individual, greater social justice, and understanding and respect for nature, and a reverence for all life. . . . We now see that our very survival is at stake if we do not use our newfound knowledge and power to translate more of our ideals into realities.

—Glenn T. Seaborg

We must look deeper than the political and economic catastrophes of the modern world if we would find the real cause of the contemporary tragedy. The cause of the tragedy is neither political nor economic. It is that the race has been induced to forget its true end through which happiness (Carlyle's blessedness) alone can come.

—Alfred Noyes

For a century man has moved ever deeper into a crisis which has much in common with others we know from earlier history, but has one essential peculiarity. This concerns man's relation to the new things and connections which have arisen by his action or with his cooperation. I should like to call this peculiarity of the modern man's crisis man's lagging behind his works. Man is no longer able to master the world which he himself has brought about: it is becoming stronger than he is, it is winning free of him, it confronts him in an almost elemental independence, and he no longer knows the word which could subdue and render harmless the golem he has created. Our age has experienced this paralysis and failure of the human soul successively in three realms. The first was the realm of technique. Machines, which were invented in order to serve men in their work, impressed him into their service. They were no longer, like tools, an extension of man's arm, but man became their extension, an adjunct on their periphery, doing their bidding. The second realm was the economic. Production, immensely increased in order to supply the growing number of men with what they needed, did not reach a reasonable coordination; it is as though the production and utilization of goods spread out beyond man's reach and withdrew itself from his command. The third realm was the political. In the first world war, and on both sides, man learned with ever greater horror how he was in the grip of incomprehensible powers, which seemed, indeed, to be connected with man's will but which threw off their bonds and again and again trampled on all human purposes, till finally they brought all, both on this side and the other, to destruction. Man faced the terrible fact that he was the father of demons whose master he could not become.

—*Martin Buber*

Certainly our contemporary world is a mess. "Everything nailed down is comin' loose," as the Angel Gabriel in *Green Pastures* said to "de Lawd." International relations, economic conditions, moral customs, are inconstant and confused. . . . Ideas, habits, institutions, ethical standards, once apparently solid and durable, now seem to many "frail as frost landscapes on a windowpane." The hydrogen bomb makes everything on earth seem perishable. . . .

This transitory aspect of our world and of our lives within it confronts us all . . . .

Life on a transient planet, in an exploding universe, with all existence the ephemeral result of colliding physical particles going it blind, is utterly meaningless. It comes from nowhere and is going nowhither. Its only continuity is the repetition of endless variation; its only changeless element is change. There is no design behind it, no purpose in it, no outcome ahead of it, and Macbeth's description of it is accurate: "full of sound and fury, signifying nothing." Only when amid this jumble of vicissitude and mutability something constant and abiding is seen, only when the eternal emerges amid the transient, is there any ultimate sense in human life, and for lack of *that* increasing numbers of people are confused and desperate. As one young collegian put it, "What is there to tie to?"

To be sure, many thoughtlessly shrug off serious consideration of life's final significance, and proceed from day to day on what passing happiness they find. But soon or late the ultimate question confronts most of us—what does life mean in a mess of a world like this? and in these days of upheaval the number of souls facing that question multiplies. . . .

Generations differ in their most urgent need. History could be written in terms of the varied intellectual and spiritual problems which, from age to age, have pressed up into the crucial focus of attention; and in our time, tottering with worldwide convulsions, this problem which we are considering is important. To find the permanent amid the impermanent, the durable amid the fugitive, is now a matter of life and death. . . .

Indeed, a chaotic era, such as ours, presents not only the *need* of discerning the abiding amid the transitory, but as well the *opportunity* of discerning it. The highest use of a shaken time is to discover the unshakable. When everything that can totter is staggering, then is the time to get our eyes on what stands firm.

—*Harry Emerson Fosdick*

We Western peoples are apt to think our great problems are external, environmental. We are not skilled in the inner life, where the real roots of our problem lie. For I would suggest that the true explanation of the complexity of our program is an inner one, not an outer one. The outer distractions of our interests reflect an inner lack of integration of our own lives. We are trying to be several selves at once, without all our selves being organized by a single, mastering Life within us. Each of us tends to be. . . a whole committee of selves. There is the civic self, the parental self, the financial self, the religious self, the society self, the professional self, the literary self. And each of our selves is in turn a rank individualist, not co-operative but shouting out his vote loudly for himself when the voting time comes. . . . We are distraught. We feel honestly the pull of many obligations and try to fulfill them all. . . .

Strained by the very mad pace of our daily outer burdens, we are further strained by an inward uneasiness, because we have hints that there is a way vastly richer and deeper than all this hurried existence, a life of unhurried serenity and peace and power.

—Thomas Kelly

We live in times of such anger and surging unrest that it is uncertain what the internal struggles of our own nation will be and what it will mean to be in the fray for justice and not flee the cities.

Yet there is something else about these times. We have grown aware that the terrible unbalances that exist in society also exist in our very beings. We have not been able to avoid seeing the feat of men on the moon against the plight of our urban centers. Every walk in moon dust illuminates in a piercing way the division and strife of earth men. We know that we have grown up lopsided. The age of the Spirit did not dawn with the age of science and technology, and the gap between the two threatens us and our kind with extinction. We possess the heights of the sky and the depths of the ocean, but the heights and the depths within are unexplored. So long as this is true we are not in possession of ourselves. Much of our violence is the rage of the dispossessed, though it may be more appropriate to say the "have nots," for many of us never did possess ourselves. We are simply the deprived who have not claimed our inheritance to use either foolishly or wisely. Everywhere the recognition breaks with new force that the unexplored, untouched shores are within.

—Elizabeth O'Connor

To our mystically inclined ancestors the world was important chiefly insofar as it furthered man's spiritual life. Now the scales have tipped toward the other extreme. Religion has become merely the more or less valued servant of material existence; and art, once the sacred messenger from superhuman realms, is seldom more than exhibitionism. . . .

In retrospect, the emergence of a materialistic era seems to have been inevitable, and thus a part of human destiny. And since materialism affected the vast majority of men, involving even those who hated and feared it, it would be more realistic to study its meaning than to condemn it as the cause of all our troubles. . . .

Our generation is in mortal danger of losing the faculty of stimulating consciousness from *within*. It takes very little self-investigation to discover that today's ceaseless striving for sensory stimulation is motivated less by a positive longing for happiness than by subconscious fear of mental collapse. The foreboding symptoms of such crises—boredom, depression, and anxiety, setting in as soon as outer stimulation ceases—indicate the barrenness which prevails in whole areas of our soul life.

—Dr. Franz E. Winkler

Each of us has to define himself for himself and we look for clues out there, in the world around us. To form an idea of our worth we study our images in the mirror of other people's eyes. For the benefit of those mirrors we cloak ourselves in all sorts of fashionable notions, status symbols, brand names, and other facades of eggshell fragility. Then we wonder why the stranger reflected back at us is unrecognizable. We've tried to invent ourselves from the outside in. We've based our hope on a bit of flash that can be bought and sold. We've wanted so desperately to be somebody that we've ended up being nobody where it counts. . . .

Impatient for results, our generation has built without foundation, choosing display over truth, and we've respected ourselves so little that we now seem hell-bent on destruction. It's an awfully religious thing to say in an irreligious age, but we have not been looking into our souls.

We've got to learn to look at the whole of ourselves, the bad and the good and the in-between, for it's all part of the mystery and the miracle of life. We all start out with this incredible gift in us. We can grow and we can learn. We are capable of compassion and hope and love. We must cherish our life for what it is, sad and gay and funny and awful and tragic and a triumph. . . .

Each hour of each day we make the small choices that add up to a lifetime. We must learn to choose those things that embrace life, and then, when we're making ourselves into somebody, it'll be somebody worth being.

—Wyatt Cooper

Men travel side by side for years, each locked up in his own silence or exchanging those words which carry no freight—till danger comes. Then they stand shoulder to shoulder. They discover that they belong to the same family. They wax and bloom in the recognition of fellow beings. They look at each other and smile. They are like the prisoner set free who marvels at the immensity of the sea.

Happiness! It is useless to seek it elsewhere than in this warmth of human relations. Our sordid interests imprison us within their walls. Only a comrade can grasp us by the hand and haul us free.

And those human relations must be created. One must go through an apprenticeship to learn the job. Games and risk are a help here. When we exchange many handshakes, compete in races, join together to save one of us who is in trouble, cry aloud for help in the hour of danger—only then do we learn that we are not alone on earth.

Each man must look to himself to teach him the meaning of life. It is not something discovered; it is something moulded. These prison walls that this age of trade has built up round us, we can break down. We can still run free, call to our comrades, and marvel to hear once more, in response to our call, the pathetic chant of the human voice.

—Antoine de Saint-Exupèry

I presume the reason that we do not discover ourselves more often than we do. . . is because of the unpleasantness which we know awaits us at the center of our being. For whenever we come to ourselves in moments of insight, when in the lightning flash of revelation we have seen what was in the darkness of our inner world, we have had a most uncomfortable experience. We are mixtures of good and evil, sometimes saint and sometimes sinner, with awful doubt and desperate faith wrestling forever in the deep abyss, and all the perennial paradoxes of death and God and love running like angry spears through the quiet heart, while the brain asks its innumerable questions, and the tongue babbles on with endless words, and the eyes busy themselves with many things, and the body is filled with its own anxieties.

Such a strange world do you and I enclose, a world of glory and shame, of tenderness and indifference, of wisdom and stupidity, of great things and mean, heroic and despicable at once. It is no wonder we flee from such contradiction, humiliation and embarrassment.

—Samuel Miller

Must fear of other men, of ourselves, forever determine our behavior? If the human creature could advance in goodwill, tolerance and self-abnegation at the same speed as he has with his scientific inventions; if he could replace his lost faith in the institutional religions with a real sense of the stake each and every member of the human race has in the human condition, then we might see a fresh flowering of the spirit of man and a redressing of the sad imbalance visible to the young, who search for values and find none, who have weighed us, the older generation, in the balance and found us wanting.

—Yehudi Menuhin

Man's development requires his capacity to transcend the narrow prison of his age, his greed, his selfishness, his separation from his fellow man, and, hence, his basic loneliness. This transcendence is the condition for being open and related to the world, vulnerable and yet with an experience of identity and integrity; of man's capacity to enjoy all that is alive, to pour out his faculties into the world around him, to be "interested"; in brief, to *be* rather than to *have* and to *use* are consequences of the step to overcome greed and egomania. . . .

The dynamism of human nature inasmuch as it is human is primarily rooted in this need of man to *express his faculties in relation to the world rather than his need to use the world as a means for the satisfaction of his physiological necessities.*

—Erich Fromm

The sudden stopping of J——— T———'s heart is a tragic loss for all of us. Others work for science, for prosperity, for education, for the welfare of the group. J——— chose to work and live for the separate happiness of every member of the company. That was his career. He devoted his days and his nights to trying to match the coldly formal needs of our group—the planning needs, the research needs, the profit needs—to the warmly human and special needs of each person who as a human being turned to him for support, understanding, courage, and guidance. All through our thirty-six hundred people it was known that if there was something you didn't understand about where you were going, or about you and your supervisor, or about you and your job, even about you and your family—you could look to J——— T——— for guidance, support, and love.

In a society so often made frigid by organization, J———T——— taught that life could be warm and fruitful if you understood yourself, loved your friends, had faith in life, and used organization not as a threat but as a tool for our common welfare.

It is a tragedy that medical science does not yet know how to care for the physical heart of a man who chose to give his whole spiritual heart to others. But we all know that even premature death cannot make J———'s life tragic because he will go on for generations in the mind and being of those for whom he lived.

It is important for his family to know of our sympathy and even more important for them to know that their support for him gave him the strength to be strong for others.

—a tribute from a company President

The very fact that one has never incurred the overt condemnation of society or fallen into the toils of the law may induce a false complacency and dull one's awareness of sin. An important reason for the chaos and meaninglessness of much of present-day life is the lack of any clear grasp of the reality of sin in its subtler forms. Not drunkenness, adultery, or theft, but self-love, self-righteousness, self-seeking, the will to power and prestige, unkindness, anger and vindictiveness, irresponsibility, complacency before the suffering of the world, wilful narrowing of vision to the interests of one's own family, community, race, or nation are among the major sins of most people. Only as a sensitive conscience on these matters is aroused can we hope for much in the way of either social salvation or the individual remaking of life.

—Georgia Harkness

Let us remember for our consolation that we never perceive our sins till we begin to cure them. We must neither flatter nor be impatient with ourselves in the correction of our faults. Despondency is not a state of humility; on the contrary, it is the vexation and despair of a cowardly pride—nothing is worse; whether we stumble or whether we fall, we must think only of rising and going on in our course.

—François de la Mothe Fénelon

Life is meant to be lived from a Center, a divine Center. Each one of us can live such a life of amazing power and peace and serenity, of integration and confidence and simplified multiplicity on one condition—that is, *if we really want to*. There is a divine Abyss within us all, a holy Infinite Center, a Heart, a Life who speaks in us and through us to the world. We have all heard this holy Whisper at times. At times we have followed the Whisper, and amazing equilibrium of life, amazing effectiveness of living set in. But too many of us have heeded the Voice only at times. Only at times have we submitted to His holy guidance. We have not counted this Holy Thing within us to be the most precious thing in the world.

–Thomas Kelly

It is through the door of the present moment that God enters into your life, and it is through you that he enters into the life of the world. But God will not step through that door unless you open it to him. Each moment is an annunciation in your life, but you can only respond to God's call if you're there to hear it. . . .

The most important and most efficacious commitment of yourself that you can make is the commitment you make . . . in the present moment by leaving to God both the past and the future and placing yourself totally at his disposal. If you are faithful to this commitment you will live your life to the full and you will make a complete success of your life in the world.

—Michel Quoist

Prayer is a force as real as terrestrial gravity. As a physician, I have seen men, after all other therapy had failed, lifted out of disease and melancholy by the serene effort of prayer. It is the only power in the world that seems to overcome the so-called "laws of nature"; the occasions on which prayer has dramatically done this have been termed "miracles." But a constant, quieter miracle takes place hourly in the hearts of men and women who have discovered that prayer supplies them with a steady flow of sustaining power in their daily lives.

Too many people regard prayer as a formalized routine of words, a refuge for weaklings, or a childish petition for material things. . . . Properly understood, prayer is a mature activity indispensable to the fullest development of personality—the ultimate integration of man's highest faculties. Only in prayer do we achieve that complete and harmonious assembly of body, mind, and spirit which gives the frail human reed its unshakable strength. . . .

How can prayer be defined? Prayer is the effort of man to reach God, to commune with an invisible being, creator of all things, supreme wisdom, truth, beauty, and strength, father and redeemer of each man. This goal of prayer always remains hidden to intelligence. For both language and thought fail when we attempt to describe God.

—Dr. Alexis Carrel

The conception of God as a lonely sovereign, complete in Himself and infinitely separated from us "poor worms of the dust" . . . is in the main a dead notion. . . . That whole conception is being supplanted by a *live faith* in an infinite person who is corporate with our lives, from whom we have sprung, in whom we live, as far as we spiritually do live, who needs us as we need Him, and who is sharing with us the travail and the tragedy as well as the glory and the joy of bringing forth sons of God.

In such a kingdom—an organic fellowship of interrelated persons—prayer is as normal an activity as gravitation in a world of matter. We are no longer in the net of blind fate, in the realm of impersonal force, we are in a love-system where the aspiration of one member heightens the entire group, and the need of one—even the least—draws upon the resources of the whole—even the Infinite. We are in actual divine-human fellowship.

—Rufus Jones

We have only to be patient, to pray, and to do his will, according to our present light and strength, and the growth of the soul will go on. The plant grows in the mist and under clouds as truly as under sunshine. So does the heavenly principle within.

—W. E. Channing

Prayer is not informing God of something he does not already know, or pleading with him to change his mind. Prayer is the opening of the soul to God so he can speak to us. "Prayer is not overcoming God's reluctance; it is laying hold of God's willingness."

It is essential to any real understanding of prayer that we get this sequence straight. God speaks, and summons us to respond. But . . . there is also in prayer communication and response in which we speak and God responds. Prayer is "the offering up of our desires unto God." This means the voicing before God of whatever is deepest within the soul with the expectation that he will hear and answer. The answer comes in many ways—in the strengthening of the inner life, in direction for action, in quieting of anxiety, in assurance of sin forgiven, in a sense of divine companionship that gives peace and power. It can come in the reshaping of events. . . . The answer does not always come as the pray-er expects or desires.

—Georgia Harkness

Prayer does not change God but it changes him who prays.

—Sören Kierkegaard

Whatsoever it is that presses thee, go tell thy Father; put over the matter into His hand, and so thou shalt be freed from that dividing, perplexing care that the world is full of. When thou art either to do or suffer anything, when thou art about any purpose or business, go tell God of it, and acquaint Him with it; yea, burden Him with it, and thou hast done for matter of caring; no more care, but quiet, sweet diligence in thy duty, and dependence on Him for the carriage of thy matters. Roll thy cares, and thyself with them, as one burden, all on thy God.

—Robert Leighton

Trust in the Lord with all thine heart, and lean not unto thine own understanding. In all thy ways acknowledge him, and he shall direct thy paths.

—Proverbs 3:5, 6

A statement of Fénelon's came to be a source of strength to me. . . . Short enough to be slipped through the mind in a few seconds before any "moment of duty or of action" this talisman sentence helps to release tension, to restore a sense of proportion. . . . "Cheered by the presence of God, I will do each moment without anxiety, according to the strength which he shall give me, the work which His Providence assigns me."

—Elizabeth Gray Vining

You may want *peace of mind* so that you can accept life. Your need is to be able to take all that life does to you. You search for an inner composure and calm that will give you an inner stability when the storms blow and sickness, sufferings, sorrows, defeats, and failures descend. Especially you may long for a peace within that overcomes all fears and anxieties. This search for peace of mind seldom has anything to do with material needs or wants. Frequently it is the most prosperous outwardly who are the most fearful inwardly. . . .

Or you may be looking for power for living. Your life seems to have gone along so far and then you have run out of gas. The tasks of creative living seem too great for you. The demands are too much. . . .

If it is not peace of mind you need, nor power for living, then you probably know your need above all other needs—to be forgiven. . . nearly all of us belong in various degrees in all three groups. The most basic need, however, ultimately bound up with the other two, is this: to be made clean. . . .

We are all in difficulty in life because we are separated from God. That separation is our sin. Once we confess our sin, God takes it away, and then we are right with him. Once we have been made clean, *then* we are given also the keys to peace of mind and power for living.

—John B. Coburn

When we try to pray in accordance with the purpose of God, we find ourselves drawn out of our self-centredness into the worship and prayer of the whole family of God for the whole family of mankind. . . . Whatever our "views," in this kind of deep prayer, we are in vital unity with all in whom flows the life of Christ, the power of the Spirit.

—Dr. Olive Wyon

To give ourselves to God is to give ourselves to Life, for God is the source and author of life. To give ourselves to Him so that all our strength, our energies, our desires become unified in a flight towards life, towards God, this is to know joy, and that joy no man can take away from us. It is something which is above the reach of circumstance.

—Dr. Agnes Maude Royden

I love them that love me, and those that seek me early shall find me.

—Proverbs 8:17

As surely as a sailing ship is made to sail with the wind, so are you and I and everybody else in this wide world over made to be bound to each other as a brother is bound to a brother, giving and receiving mercy, binding up each other's wounds, taking care of each other. If we really look at our own lives, seeing not what we expect them to be, but what they are, we cannot help seeing that. Nobody can. It need not have been so. It can be imagined otherwise. We might have been made to live on self-interest or solitude or pure reason. Yet it is so.

—Frederick Buechner

To me humanity is like a great orchestra created by God to learn the music of the holy Will, and sin is the discordant note that always spoils the perfect harmony. All the difficulties and struggles are the practising school in which we are learning to play our part.

—W. F. Adams, S.S.J.E. and Gilbert Shaw

It is our relation with God which invests our lives with . . . a dignity which demands "that every human being should be treated as a responsible human person, with rights and duties, an inner sacrosanct life, as well as a community life." If we are unaware of the responsibility of human life, it is in prayer that we learn our dignity as the "dear children of God." And it is in prayer, as co-operation with the will of God, that we learn how deeply our lives affect other lives, and through them, the whole life of society. Father D'Arcy insists that this truth is frequently neglected, and that we are "scarcely ever told that by our own personal decision the lives of countless persons living and to come will be affected, and the splendor of our unique life achieved. Yet this is true. . . .

". . . life is full of meaning, and this end, which is the purpose of God, is one to which by our prayers, our self-offering, our actions, we can contribute. To see this, and to try, however imperfectly, to live by it, fills our lives with a deep satisfaction. Through our relation with God as personal beings we find we are achieving our destiny."

—Dr. Olive Wyon

God alone knows
what He expects of us,
what response He's looking for
and how many people's destinies depend on ours.
When we scorn ourselves,
we scorn all those plans of His,
all the dreams He was going to realize through us,
all the joy He anticipated from us
and all the hope He's placed in us.
Each of us is a piece of property
that belongs to God
but is entrusted to us.
We hardly ever know of what use it is,
and, as a rule, He's careful not to tell us.
Quite naturally, we often wonder
what it can possibly be for

and who or what can ever really benefit
from our life.
Faith makes us believe
that God deems it useful,
necessary for His projects
and indispensable to His joy.

—*Louis Evely*

Religious faith which springs out of the vision of transcendent Reality and an ultimate divine purpose is a stabilizing power of the first importance, for health of body as well as for peace of mind. It not only stabilizes one's life; it beautifies and consecrates it. It infuses a marching power. It liberates and lifts. It opens windows and doors of a person's life for action and is essentially a dynamic of action. It enlarges perspective and it makes one feel himself to be a citizen of an enlarged universe—a two-storied world to which he belongs, the upper story as real as the basic material one.

—*Rufus Jones*

THE CHALLENGE TO GROW

He said not:
Thou shalt not be tempested,
Thou shalt not be travailed,
Thou shalt not be afflicted;
But He said:
Thou shalt not be overcome.

—Dame Julian of Norwich

A GUIDE FOR ALL WEATHERS

Some time in life, riding one's self-chosen road to the world-famous city of Success, everyone runs into trouble of one sort or another. I presume you have or you wouldn't be reading this book.

Sometimes the "car" breaks down or shows alarming signs of wear at high speed. Its engine seems to lack power for getting you up steep slopes, or its brakes prove faulty on some dangerous curve along the way. Alcohol won't fix it, you discover.

Or, while bowling happily along, you find a roadblock barring further progress—no sign! Is this barrier temporary or worse? World-shaking events, an economic depression, inflation, loss of a good job, an accident, illness, serious family problems, the dissolution of a marriage-partnership—all can be such roadblocks.

If you aren't stopped by a barrier, you come to a fork. Again, no sign. Which road will take you where you want to go? God knows! Even an unbeliever in that fix may cry out, "Show me the way!" and find that the route he is led to take brings him at last to a shining God-governed realm where the deepest needs of his spirit are fulfilled.

I share with you a jotting from my notebook, the words of an American woman novelist who has since died: "Every crucial experience can be regarded as a setback—or the start of a new kind of development."

I add another from a father who had suffered deeply, the words taken from a letter to his children: "When you understand what you see, you will no longer be children. You will know that life is pain, and that each of us hangs always upon the cross of himself. And when you know that this is true of every man, woman and child on earth, you will be wise."

I think it was a Swiss doctor who once wrote that every dilemma can be solved only at a deeper level. I have found that to be true again and again when I prayed in days of trouble, "Show me the way you want me to take" or "Reveal the solution to this difficult problem."

As rings of growth are clearly visible in a cross-section of a great sequoia, so each of us is aware of growth experiences in our past, incised into our being by trouble. As I look back, I can see that it was my daring leap of trust—the ultimate commitment of all my weaknesses and "gifts," all I was and longed to be, made to the Holy Spirit when I was threatened with defeat—that was responsible for every blessing the later years have brought.

If you can't go on in the direction you chose, you are bound to discover in time what you were meant to do and be, simply by asking daily for God's guidance. If you offer yourself to the Source of Life, "bestower of every good and perfect gift," as a channel for his *outreach of Love, you will grow in wisdom and understanding and become a blessing and source of strength to all whom your life touches.*

Dorothy Mason Fuller

It is a tremendous moment when first one is called upon to join the great army of those who suffer.

That vast world of love and pain opens suddenly to admit us one by one within its fortress. We are afraid to enter into the land, yet you will, I know, feel how high is the call. It is as a trumpet speaking to us, that cries aloud—"It is your turn—endure." Play your part. As they endured before you, so now, close up the ranks —be patient and strong as they were. Since Christ, this world of pain is no accident, untoward or sinister, but a lawful department of life, with experiences, interests, adventures, hopes, delights, secrets of its own. These are all thrown open to us as we pass within the gates— things that we could never learn or know or see, so long as we were well.

God help you to walk through this world now opened to you as through a kingdom, regal, royal, and wide and glorious.

—Henry Scott Holland

Life only demands from you the strength you possess. Only one feat is possible—not to have run away.

—Dag Hammarskjöld

There are few road maps, and there should be few, to guide a man who faces suffering as a new experience.

The way ahead is essentially unknown for each sufferer and because of the individuality of each human person the way has to be clarified through his own experience. This can cause great fears at the outset. It can cause a man to play roles, to assume masks of bravery, courage, patience, even when such masks are alien to the reality the sufferer experiences within himself. Because he is in unfamiliar territory, the sufferer naturally assumes attitudes he thinks society expects and admires. Before suffering itself can clarify values for him, he begins to search frantically for the reasons for his suffering. . . .

The mind seeks reasons for what is happening to the body, and so the mind grasps at these "reasons" even while the body casts them into doubt. The body can even lead men to suspect that there are no reasons, that it just happened, that the pain is going to "evaporate uselessly."

Only later, and usually in ways quite different from the expected or hoped-for ones, does the realization come that a transformation has occurred—a massive transformation—the effects of which begin to manifest themselves even while the causes remain obscure; and the man who has suffered deeply can see in these effects that nothing was, in fact, wasted.

—*John Howard Griffin*

How wonderful it is . . . that literally only Christianity has taught us the true peace and function of suffering. The Stoics tried the hopeless little game of denying its objective reality, or of declaring it a good in itself (which it never is), and the Pessimists tried to revel in it as a food to their melancholy and as something that can no more be transformed than it can be avoided or explained. But Christ came and He did not really explain it; He did far more, He met it, willed it, transformed it, and He taught us how to do all this, or rather He himself does it within us, if we do not hinder His all-healing hands. . . . In suffering we are very near to God.

We cannot really . . . stand it properly, for half an hour; and God will and does give us His grace to stand it for as long as ever He chooses, provided we will, according to the intensity of the trial, contract our outlook to the day, or the hour, or even the minute. God, the essentially timeless, will thus and then help His poor timeful creature to contract time to a point of most fruitful faith and love.

—Baron Friedrich von Hügel
(from letters to a friend in her last illness)

God speaks to us all the time. He has always spoken to us in his language, in the severe and simple language of our daily existence. We do not hear him because we would like him to speak to us in ours, in our language of happiness such as we imagine it, through poor and silly satisfactions of feeling, self-love, or even comfort, the only messages that we have decided to recognize as his.

But God speaks to us with perseverance in his language, God speaks to us in this language, unknown to us and which we are reluctant to learn, of acceptance, of sacrifice, of renunciation, the language of a prodigiously far-reaching, incredibly generous plan through which he wants to save us, and the world. God speaks to us unceasingly through the events of our life, through his obstinacy in thwarting our petty human plans, through his punctuality in disappointing our projects and our attempts to escape, through the perpetual failure of all our calculations to manage to do without him. And little by little he tames us, he familiarizes us. One day when we are confined to our bed, checkmated by a failure, isolated by a misfortune, annihilated by the feeling of our powerlessness, one day, he resigns us to listen to his language, to admit his presence, to acknowledge his will. And we know then that he was speaking to us all the time.

—*Louis Evely*

Sickness and suffering are somewhat like a great windstorm in a forest. The dead trees are downed, the forest thinned out, dead branches fall, and the trees remaining have a better chance to grow. The storm improves the forest. Often the dead timber in human life falls away during illness, and one emerges a better person. The dead branches of pettiness and selfishness fall off. The trees of true value stand taller.

Sickness and suffering teach us many lessons. They bring new insights, sharpen perceptions, give a new scale of values, aid perspective, shake a person out of his complacency, cause him to appreciate life's simple gifts, widen the horizon of knowledge of human experience, and bring into bold relief life's essentials.

—Edmond Holt Babbitt

I wish you could convince yourself that God is often nearer to us, and more effectually present with us, in sickness than in health.

—Brother Lawrence

If there is something going on behind the screen of outward events and this great impulse of redemptive love is forever besieging us, why are we not more open to its guidance? There is an old story of a small boy who was puzzling over Holman Hunt's great painting that shows the figure of Jesus knocking at the door of a house—a weed-clogged door that is only able to be opened from the inside. The child asked his father why the people didn't open the door, and then with a cry of discovery he gave his own answer. "I think I know why they don't open the door. They're all down in the basement and they don't hear him."

The basement where the gentle knocking is inaudible is expressive of the human condition as we know it today. . . . It seems for many to take shattering experiences to rouse them to what is already going on. Phillips Brooks, who had no gift for keeping discipline, was literally run out of his first job at the Boston Latin School. It was only out of a long breakdown that there emerged for him a call to prepare himself for the ministry. Thomas Kelly had a crushing blow to his academic ambitions dealt to him in the autumn of 1937 and he went through a time of brokenness and despair. Out of it came a whole new level of awareness of what was going on and the surge of new life which the *Testament of Devotion* shares with our generation.

For some it is the running away from home of a precious child, or the loss of a secure post, or the breakdown in mental or physical health, or the loss of a wife or a husband or a child through death that breaks through the hard hull of self-assurance. W. H. Auden has a line which says, "It is where we are wounded that God speaks to us." Auden does not say that God sends these wounds. But he seems to be saying that for some of us it is only in the depths of suffering that we seem open enough to listen to what, upon the occasion of this suffering, God has to say to us. "Behold, I stand at the door and knock."

—Douglas Steere

Those who suffer are altered. Whatever the reason, it is already something to have one foot out of this ignoble security. Those who suffer are the witnesses in the world of the crying need of God.

—Louis Evely

Pain and suffering draw out from us the latent spiritual powers which we have. Just as physical abilities are developed by exercise and meeting obstacles, so spiritual muscles are strengthened by facing suffering. An engineer will quickly say that no progress is made in the world of engineering without friction. Friction is also necessary in human life. We grow as we meet obstacles. Every person is a potential conqueror over hardship, grief, disaster, and suffering. Live fish swim against the stream; dead fish float. . . .

For years E. Stanley Jones has maintained that the Christian way to face suffering is to use it. We believe it is not the direct will of God that we suffer, yet when we are called upon to suffer, we ought to learn the lessons it has to teach.

—Edmond Holt Babbitt

Adversity has the effect of eliciting talents, which, in prosperous circumstances, would have lain dormant.

—Horace

Pain makes man think. Thought makes man wise. Wisdom makes life endurable.

—John Patrick

Physical suffering, if the sufferer allows it to do with him what it can—in a kind of simplicity and openness to its teachings—turns the sufferer into giver, into lover, into consoler. Long experience with physical suffering has taught him that he can bear what he has borne. But he cannot bear it when others suffer. It constantly reawakens him to mercy and to an authentic pity which bring in their wake a melting of the callouses of indifference and unconcern for others. Even the man totally immobilized and locked in pain, *the moment all elements of self-pity have evaporated,* can spread an authentic and curative pity that sometimes seems to blaze from him.

—John Howard Griffin

Nothing happens to any man which he is not formed by nature to bear.

—Marcus Aurelius

To strive with difficulties and to conquer them, is the highest human felicity.

—Samuel Johnson

Success is to be reckoned, I believe, in what a man can endure or in what a man can learn, certainly not in what a man can possess. . . . Nor is happiness any test of a life well and truly lived. . . . No, we were not born merely for that. Ours is a higher destiny. "Happinesses, whether temporal or eternal, are not the reward man seeks," writes R. L. Stevenson, "his soul is on the journey." . . .

If in truth this earth of ours in its main purpose is what Keats called it—"a vale of soul-making," then certainly we must be prepared to "take our share of hardship." A self-centred life nearly always charges God with carelessness and lovelessness when the road turns uphill, when pain and suffering, loss or disappointment are companions of the journey.

"Why should this come upon me?" people complain. . . . They have been respectable folk; they have done their best for their children. . . . Then why on earth should they suffer? . . . with no idea that there are deep truths that only suffering can teach; that to suffer in body is often to grow in spirit; that our real progress can only be measured by the quality of our lives; that in any case there are many sufferings and temptations that are common to man. It is upon no velvet anvil that the soul of man can be forged.

—W. H. Elliott

Life is creative strife. It takes the adverse strands and weaves them into the fabric of character.

—Charles H. Brent

An active life serves the purpose of giving man the opportunity to realize values in creative work, while a passive life of enjoyment affords him the opportunity to obtain fulfillment in experiencing beauty, art, or nature. But there is also purpose in that life which is almost barren of both creation and enjoyment and which admits of but one possibility of high moral behavior: namely, in man's attitude to his existence, an existence restricted by external forces. A creative life and a life of enjoyment are banned to him. But not only creativeness and enjoyment are meaningful. If there is a meaning in life at all, then there must be a meaning in suffering. Suffering is an ineradicable part of life, even as fate and death. Without suffering and death human life cannot be complete.

The way in which a man accepts his fate and all the sufferings it entails . . . gives him ample opportunity—even under the most difficult circumstances—to add a deeper meaning to his life. It may remain brave, dignified and unselfish. . . .

Everywhere man is confronted with fate, with the chance of achieving something through his own suffering.

—*Dr. Viktor E. Frankl*

The soul loses command of itself when it is impatient. Whereas, when it submits without a murmur it possesses itself in peace, and possesses God. To be impatient, is to desire what we have not, or not to desire what we have. When we acquiesce in an evil, it is no longer such. Why make a real calamity of it by resistance? Peace does not dwell in outward things, but within the soul. We may preserve it in the midst of the bitterest pain, if one remains firm and submissive. Peace in this life springs from acquiescence even in disagreeable things, not in an exemption from bearing them.

—François de la Mothe Fénelon

There is always a radiance in the soul of man, untroubled like the light in a lantern in a wild turmoil of wind and tempest.

—Plotinus

God does not die on the day we cease to believe in a personal deity, but we die on the day when our lives cease to be illumined by the steady radiance, renewed daily, of a wonder, the source of which is beyond all reason.

—Dag Hammarskjöld

God brings every man to a moment in his life when there takes place within him—often over some quite minor act of obedience—this inner debate as to which of . . . two attitudes—resistance or acceptance—he is to adopt. This moment cannot be artificially created, nor can it be escaped when it comes. . . .

The solemn moment of decision sometimes comes on

the occasion of an illness, which one sees as a warning sent from God; or of a moral conflict, which shows up the disorder in one's mind. But this renunciation is quite as necessary in the healthiest and most evenly balanced lives, for no man does it by nature. Sometimes it is quite a simple matter, and seems to be given by grace, and sometimes it is a heroic struggle. Sometimes it results from quite orthodox preaching; sometimes it happens amid dogmatic assertions, the error of which one later recognizes; sometimes it is helped by something said by a person with no pretentions whatever to religion. It matters little how one finds God, or that the field in which the discovery is made is a limited one. The experience is always accompanied by the feeling that something absolutely new has come into one's life. It is in substance a new quality of life which will gradually penetrate all other fields of one's activity. We are sometimes put off by the immense complexity of human problems, as if one had to deal with every fruit on a tree separately in order to ripen it. Now at last we realize that all we have to do is to plant the tree, water it, and protect it against parasites, in order to have each fruit ripening of itself in its own proper time.

One of my patients writes: "I remember that an important decision—to give up a love affair—had at once made all my other feelings and thoughts clearer. Until then I had been sick with indecision in every department of my life."

One further point is that this decision, while it brings new life and hope, does come into collision with one's old, ingrained habits, and the repetition of this reversal causes new habits to be substituted for the old.

So the reversal is qualitatively total from the first. It is God that is found, not "a little bit of God," whenever the heart turns toward him. But the new attitude, which is contained virtually in the first act of obedience, is only realized through a continual examination of the conscience.

—Dr. Paul Tournier

Human wisdom is quite impressive until the shadow of death appears, and that shadow appears whenever pain strikes. Think of all the knowledge in the university down the street: it is wonderful until . . . until we are on a hospital bed, not at all sure that we shall leave the hospital alive. Similarly human skill, as in a jet plane or a nuclear submarine, seems almost god-like until . . . until pain strikes. Then we know that even the best medical skill is finally defeated, for the doctor loses every patient at last, and the patient loses every doctor. . . .

Consider what science now calls cosmic evolution, vast explosions of hydrogen in the far incredible reaches of space, with new galaxies emerging from the flaming vortex. . . . Is all this the work of a Personal Hand?

Where is he? Beyond space and time? . . . In us? Yes, or we would not worship, and could not worship without Mystery. Yet not merely within us, dying as we die? No. Then where and how? Pain drives us into that unknown, away from our safe shore.

—George A. Buttrick

Whenever one is confronted with an inescapable, unavoidable situation, whenever one has to face a fate that cannot be changed, e.g., an incurable disease, such as an inoperable cancer, just then is one given a last chance to actualize the highest value, to fulfill the deepest meaning, the meaning of suffering. For what matters above all is the attitude we take toward suffering, the attitude in which we take our suffering upon ourselves. . . .

It is one of the basic tenets of logotherapy that man's main concern is not to gain pleasure or to avoid pain, but rather to see a meaning in his life. That is why man is even ready to suffer, on the condition, to be sure, that his suffering has a meaning. . . .

There are situations in which one is cut off from the opportunity to do one's work or to enjoy one's life; but what never can be ruled out is the unavoidability of suffering. In accepting this challenge to suffer bravely, life has a meaning up to the last moment.

—Dr. Viktor E. Frankl

Not only action, but also suffering is a way to freedom. In suffering, the deliverance consists in our being allowed to put the matter out of our own hands into God's hands. In this sense death is the crowning of human freedom.

—Dietrich Bonhoeffer

In order to be happy, we have to submit our individual will to the sovereignty of the universal will, and to feel in truth that it is our own will. When we reach that state wherein the adjustment of the finite in us to the infinite is made perfect, then pain itself becomes a valuable asset. . . .

The most important lesson that man can learn from his life is not that there *is* pain in this world, but that it depends upon him to turn it into good account, that it is possible for him to transmute it into joy. . . . It can be made so only when we realize that our individual self is not the highest meaning of our being, that in us we have the world-man who is immortal, who is not afraid of death or sufferings; and who looks upon pain as only the other side of joy.

—Rabindranath Tagore

The Old and New Testament are the words, stories and prayers of men who suffer. They do not try to hide the fact that they suffer. They find suffering integral to life. They resist it, petition God to remove it, question it, endure it, rebel against it, accept it. As they wrestle with their suffering they find they wrestle with their Lord. Something happens to them—something as radical as new birth. The burden of their message does not become suffering but change—transformation. . . .

Suffering has the possibility of stabbing us awake. It shakes us out of accustomed ways so that we see ourselves as we are, powerless to change, yet needing change. But how does it come, this "new" that we must have?

Suffering can drive us deep into ourselves where, not on the surface of our lives, but at the center of being we ask the question, "Who am I? From where do I come and where am I going?" He who asks these questions stands in the way of receiving an answer. . . . Suffering has the possibility of enabling us to bring all of our many selves under the Lordship of the Father. A power comes to those who are under this authority. They possess themselves. This is their sonship with the Father. No authority in the external structures of the world can take away the authority of such persons.

—Elizabeth O'Connor

The discovery that you have cancer is also the discovery that you are going to die. Not necessarily from this cancer, this operation, for you may still live to die of heart disease or falling down the cellar stairs. But the message now comes home, strange and familiar: I too am mortal.

By necessity then you are led to meditation, even if you have not been much given to it before. In the long dark hours after the hospital has quieted down, in the period when a half-departed anesthesia has left your mind almost suspended and separated from your body, and in the surge of new life that comes with recuperation there are rich opportunities for facing what you have to face, savoring all that memory brings you as its gift, and knowing more clearly than ever before what you want to do with the rest of your life.

—Bradford Smith

There is nothing that the body suffers that the soul may not profit by.

—George Meredith

In the midst of winter, I finally learned that there was in me an invincible summer.

—Albert Camus

Man's suffering is twofold. He suffers from the trials that are sent him, from the blows which fate deals him, from death, illness, privations, treachery, solitude, disillusionment, and so on, and so on. And he suffers, too, from rebelling against suffering, from refusing to bear it and from cursing it. And there is another and bitterer kind of suffering. When man accepts suffering and recognizes that it has a meaning, the pain grows less, becomes more endurable, and a light begins to shine through it. Unenlightened suffering, the most terrible of all, is that which man does not accept, against which he rebels and feels vindictive. But when he accepts suffering as having a higher meaning, it regenerates him. . . . Suffering tracks our steps, even the happiest of us. There is only one way open to man, the way of light and regeneration—to accept suffering as the cross which everyone must bear, following the Crucified. This is the deepest mystery of Christianity and of Christian ethics. Suffering is bound up with sin and evil, just as death is–the last of man's trials. But it is also the way of redemption, of light and regeneration. Such is the Christian paradox with regard to suffering and it must be accepted and lived through.

–Nicholas Berdyaev

Every man covets the opportunity to take the measure of his life and be able to pronounce the judgment, "It is good." And it is only to the degree that we are able to forge the diverse moments of pain and pleasure, emptiness and fulness, loneliness and love, and failure and success into some meaningful and gracious whole that we are able to escape the resentment and bitterness which form the roots of gnosticism, neurosis and despair. Finally, the most significant index we have of the stature of a man is the amount of pain and tragedy he has been able to bear and still rejoice in the gift of life.

—Sam Keen

Mental depression is often the aching of an unused faculty. It is a salutary pain, warning us that there is something wrong with our plan of life. . . . You who suffer from it, look on it as a driving force, which may be and should be used to force your life forward. . . . Do not brood; do not fret; but think the matter out. There is something in me which complains and grumbles: what does it want? It wants to have the joy of creation and achievement; what can I do to satisfy this craving? If you will use your attacks of depression in this way, they will drive you forward in a way which is impossible to the bovine, contented temperament, which takes life as it comes. . . . Make your depression a steppingstone to a richer joy; that is what God meant it to be; that is why he sent it to you.

—W. R. Inge

Paul's great conviction you know—"all things work together for good to them that love God." Is that not possessed of the same wisdom as the orchardist who knows that the soft air of spring and the bitter winds of winter would have their parts in the maturing of the fruit—a wisdom that knows there will be a harvest in spite of blight and bugs?

Many an individual who looks back on what were once considered tragic hours sees that they made possible some of the best of all experiences. The hardships of boyhood have steeled many a person for great manhood. Sorrow can leave the distillation of sympathy and humility. Defeat can strengthen resolutions. Failures can make for a wisdom that sets one on the right way to ultimate victory. Physical pain can be a rugged experience, but there can be learned the lessons of resignation, faith, and gentleness that make for spiritual healing. The calamity of death can be a sobering call to make life generous and charming. Every tragedy can be beneficial. Paul doesn't limit his proposition. "All things—the evil, disagreeable, mournful, shocking, odious, cruel—all—work for good!"

—Lowell Russell Ditzen

If we were well accustomed to the exercise of *the presence of* God, all bodily diseases would be much alleviated thereby. God often permits that we should suffer a little to purify our souls and oblige us to continue *with Him.*

Take courage: offer Him your pains incessantly: pray to Him for strength to endure them. Above all, get a habit of entertaining yourself often with God, and forget Him the least you can. Adore Him in your infirmities, offer yourself to Him from time to time, and in the height of your sufferings, beseech Him humbly and affectionately (as a child his father) to make you conformable to His holy will. . . .

God has many ways of drawing us to Himself. He sometimes hides Himself from us, but *faith* alone, which will not fail us in time of need, ought to be our support, and the foundation of our confidence, which must be all in God.

—Brother Lawrence

Faith is the soul's insight or discovery of some Reality that enables a man to stand anything that can happen to him in the universe.

—Josiah Royce

What is unbearable is not to suffer but to be afraid of suffering. To endure a precise pain, a definite loss, a hunger for something one knows—this is possible to bear. One can live with this pain. But in fear there is all the suffering of the world; to dread suffering is to suffer an infinite pain since one supposes it unbearable, it is to revolt against the universe, to lose one's place and one's rights in it, to become vulnerable over the whole extent of one's being.

—Louis Evely

You gain strength, courage, and confidence by every experience in which you really stop to look fear in the face. You are able to say to yourself, "I lived through this horror. I can take the next thing that comes along." . . . *You must do the thing you think you cannot do.*

—*Eleanor Roosevelt*

The first step toward individual conquest of fear is to recognize it as an instinctive and unreasoning reaction at whose heart lies only the same old panic that stampeded the caveman in the remote past; the transmutation of fear into courage then can be accomplished by each person in his or her own way, either by the use of common sense, intelligence, will-power or faith, or by a combination of these instinct-controlling attributes.

—*E. B. Prouty*

Most of the supremely great psalms have come out of great agonies, as the Book of Job did. Many of them, and not just one, came out of *de profundis*. Sometimes the opening verse or verses express the profound conclusion, the everlasting foundation for the soul, as the later verses of the psalm present the tragic situation which confronts the psalmist. And the psalm often closes on the same high note with which it opened. One of the reasons why these lyric cries have spoken so powerfully to the heart of the world is the fact that these beloved psalmists have trodden the paths of life before us and have sounded the deeps that are common to all humanity. Best of all they have found the eternal foundation and speak to the ages out of their depth of experience.

—*Rufus Jones*

Have mercy upon me, O Lord, for I am in trouble: mine eye is consumed with grief, yea, my soul and my belly.

For my life is spent with grief, and my years with sighing: my strength faileth because of mine iniquity, and my bones are consumed.

—Psalm 31:9, 10

God is our refuge and strength, a very present help in trouble.

—Psalm 46:1

In every pain let this thought be present, that there is no dishonor in it, nor does it make the governing intelligence worse.

Indeed, in the case of most pains, let this remark of Epicurus aid thee, that pain is neither intolerable nor everlasting—if thou bearest in mind that it has its limits, and if thou addest nothing to it in imagination.

Pain is either an evil to the body (then let the body say what it thinks of it!)—or to the soul. But it is in the power of the soul to maintain its own serenity and tranquillity, and not to think that pain is an evil. . . .

It will suffice thee to remember as concerning pain . . . that the mind may by stopping all manner of commerce and sympathy with the body, still retain its own tranquillity.

—Marcus Aurelius

Whenever evil befalls us, we ought to ask ourselves, after the first suffering, how we can turn it into good. So shall we take occasion, from one bitter root, to raise many flowers.

—Leigh Hunt

The Christian who finds himself unable to pray when sick and wanting to do so, is merely aware of the inadequacy of human language in the presence of God. At times of distress there is no need to find a form of words for our petitions. Indeed, the attempt to do so can be an unsettling failure. If we cry unto the Lord, He hears us and knows exactly the manner in which we are seeking Him, and all our needs.

With our finite minds we cannot reason about any of the worthwhile things of life or death. Spiritual strength will grow, no matter what sickness afflicts us, if we will but listen for the Voice which says: "Be still, and know that I am God."

—A. E. Gould and Vernon Symonds

When darkness is upon you, say, "This darkness is dawn not yet born; and though night's travail be full upon me, yet shall dawn be born unto me even as unto the hills."

—Kahlil Gibran

God does not punish men. Men punish themselves. God does not send misfortune and chastisements. The wickedness of men suffices to explain evil. Far from wanting to avenge himself on us, God weeps over our crimes and their consequences on us and on our descendants. . . .

Let us not look for a divine *origin* of suffering: "What have I done to God that he sends me this trial?", but for a divine *use*: "How can I make of it an act of faith and love?"

—*Louis Evely*

Health and happiness were part of the divine plan for mankind. Suffering is not the absolute will of God, as may be seen in the many miracles of healing by our Lord, and His own frequent insistence upon joy in His teaching. . . . Common sense demands that suffering should be alleviated where possible, and that in illness healing should be asked for and accepted thankfully.

But there are cases, mental and physical, which healing cannot reach. Then the lives thus touched and even dominated by pain can only be regarded as called mysteriously to suffering, and if lived in union with Him who suffered as King and Victim, they can become part of His great sacrifice.

—*W. F. Adams, S.S.J.E. and Gilbert Shaw*

One of my closest friends was a woman extremely ill with cancer. She had trained herself in the discipline of positive thinking and firm affirmation. But sometimes, she told me, the pain became so great that her affirmations and courageous will did not seem to help. I told her that at times of great pain we should not strain ourselves with the resistance of reason. At such times we should surrender ourselves like a child into the arms of the Savior, not straining upward, but letting his strong compassionate strength reach out to us. It is not we who by our faith and strength hold on to him, but rather he who keeps his hold on us. Call on him, and lean on him trustfully, knowing he has not sent us this pain, and is willing to release us from it. If we cannot pray, we can repeat inwardly some scriptural phrase that helps us, such as "Around us are the everlasting arms." We should not be too shy to ask the help of a prayer group at such times.

—Flora Slosson Wuellner

Cast thy burden upon the Lord and he shall sustain thee: He shall never suffer the righteous to be moved.

—Psalm 55:22

He shall call upon me and I will answer him: I will be with him in trouble: I will deliver him and honor him.

—Psalm 91:15

Every act of joyful acceptance of our sufferings for the love of God releases a power in the world that helps all men carry their crosses. Each such act sets free one more channel for the power of God in the lives of men, so that there is released an access of strength for every person who is carrying on his own battle against temptation or sin or suffering.

—*John B. Coburn*

Christ's way led to the cross, but it did not end there. No truth has been proved more conclusively through nearly two thousand years of history than that Christ lived on and still lives on today. He is the assurance that his way leads to life, in the kingdom of God which will never end.

—*Edith Hamilton*

Commend all to God, and then lie still and be at rest in His bosom. Whatever happens, abide steadfast in a determination to cling simply to God, trusting to His eternal love for you.

—*François de Sales*

God does not protect us against catastrophes. He is neither a lightning rod nor a breakwater. But he comes to our aid in catastrophes. It is in the very midst of the tempest and the misfortune that a wonderful zone of peace, serenity, and joy bursts in upon us, if we dwell in his grace. God does not help us before we have helped ourselves. God does not relieve us before we have exhausted our own strength. But when we are at the end of our resources, when everything is going the worst, when everything is taking place as if he did not exist or could not do anything, at this moment he manifests himself, and we begin to know that he has been there all along. . . .

Your powerlessness, your total misery will make your liberation. You will learn then that existence is a gratuitous gift and not an anxious personal industry. And the intensity of the hope which will bloom so simply in your heart will reveal to you the violence with which you had repressed it until then.

—Louis Evely

Be still awhile from thy own thoughts, searching, seeking, desires, imaginations, and be stayed on the principle of God in thee, that it may raise thy mind up to God, and stay it upon God; and thou wilt find strength from Him, and find Him to be a God at hand, a present help in time of trouble and need.

—George Fox

If in spite of all conflicts, weakness, sufferings, sins, we open our door, the spirit is poured out within us and the first mark of its presence is not an increase of energy but joy and peace. . . .

Real love always heals fear and neutralizes egotism, and so, as love grows up in us, we shall worry about ourselves less and less, and admire and delight in God and His other children more and more, and this is the secret of joy.

We shall no longer strive for our own way, but commit ourselves, easily and simply, to God's way, acquiesce in His will and in so doing, find our peace. And bit by bit there grows up in us a quiet but ardent spiritual life, tending to God, resting in God. Peace and joy are necessarily permanent characteristics of true spiritual life, the signs of God's abiding presence in the soul.

—Evelyn Underhill

Thou wilt keep him in perfect peace whose mind is stayed on thee.

—Isaiah 26:3

Father, into thy hands I commend my spirit.

—Luke 23:46

Nothing in life lasts—not even pain; this thought is comforting.

When life circumscribes and establishes painful new limitations, may it not drive us down into deeper springs of understanding? Not being able to go abroad, may we not go deep? Go high?

—David Grayson

We are apt to call things by wrong names. We will have Prosperity to be Happiness, and Adversity to be

Misery, though that is the school of Wisdom and oftentimes the way to Eternal Happiness.

—William Penn

Rejoice to think that after having recovered yourself in the midst of interior pain and difficulty, you will be able to help others in their turn. No one can help save him who has suffered. God destines you for this. Let this be your joy.

—Abbé de Tourville

No one on earth can help our pain as can those who themselves have suffered it . . . because they speak with authority. They did not choose pain nor "poison their own wine with bitter herbs when God had made it sweet." Pain chose them. If they can trust God still—if they can walk steadfastly bearing their cross—if they can still live as though life were worth living, so can we. When our turn comes to cry, "How can I bear this? How can I live through it?" and we are told "Christ bore it," we fiercely answer, "But He was God . . . how can I bear it who am a man?"—then only those whose pain is like ours . . . can answer us: . . . "I can tell you for I have borne it." . . .

Instinctively we turn to them and drink courage from their cup of pain. Their heart's blood is the wine of humanity, from which it drinks and is strong. They do not know how we live on them and by them, but it is true that—

> "Through such souls alone
> God, stooping, shows sufficient of his light
> For us in the dark to rise by. And we rise."

—Dr. Agnes Maude Royden

What a strange paradox our life is! We dread tragedy, we deplore and abhor it, and yet there is nothing on earth which we admire more than a character that handles it triumphantly. One scene I wish I could have witnessed—the convocation at the University of Glasgow when Helen Keller was given an honorary doctorate. There she stood, one of the most pitiably handicapped and yet one of the most radiant and useful personalities of her generation, while the award was given, the national anthem was sung, and her companion spelled into her hand the story of what was going on. Later, through the lips of her companion she made a brief response, thanking them for "a deed of generosity from the masters of knowledge and light to those who live under the covert of denial." These were her closing words: "Darkness and silence need not bar the progress of the immortal spirit."... It is a mysterious paradox that while we deplore Helen Keller's calamity, we admire beyond the power of words to express the spirit with which she has handled it.

—Harry Emerson Fosdick

My English friend, John Wilhelm Rowntree (1869-1905) had a unique experience in his early life. Just as he was entering young manhood and was beginning to feel the dawning sense of a great mission before him, he discovered that he was slowly losing his sight and hearing. His London doctor told him that before middle life he would become totally blind and deaf, as the result of an insidious disease. Dazed and overwhelmed, he staggered from the doctor's office to the street and stood there quite overwhelmed with the report of his condition. Suddenly he felt the love of God wrap him about as though a visible presence enfolded him, and a joy filled him such as he had never known. From that time . . . he was a gloriously joyous and happy man.

—Rufus Jones

Adjustment to blindness is very largely a matter of passing by the things you can no longer enjoy, and enjoying to the full the many things that are still yours.

—Lord Fraser of Lonsdale

I understand exactly how you feel about the power of prayer. How I wish I could find the way to get people to realize it! Realize it in the every-day problems of life and not merely in times of "extremis." I was upheld by the prayer of others to such an extent that I honestly claim to have faced the operation and afterwards without the slightest qualm, and I was never a courageous fellow. Since then I have been living constantly near the Presence of Christ, to an extent that was impossible when I was working. I have prayed for strength for my Music Hall shows—this would shock a good many—but I have been allowed to prove to myself that I can do the impossible when acting as a "pipe."

. . . in my present position [May 1961] it is comparatively easy to quest and experience the Inner Life. I no longer have to hurry over anything. My wants are miraculously supplied. . . . I find there is at least one good thing in every day. . . .

Thousands of times I have proved to be true, "Thou wilt keep him in perfect peace, whose mind is stayed on Thee."

—*A. E. Gould and Vernon Symonds*

Fairly early in his career, Beethoven felt the darkening shadows of his inevitable deafness. At first he was in despair. . . . "What a sorrowful life I must now live," he wrote; "How happy would I be if my hearing were completely restored . . . but as it is I must draw back from everything and the most beautiful years of my life will take wings without accomplishing all the promise of my talent and my powers!" So it looked and, what is more, so it would have turned out, had it not been for something else inside Beethoven. "There is no greater joy for me than to pursue and produce my art," he wrote in another letter; "Oh, if I were only rid of this affliction I could embrace the world! . . . I will seize fate by the throat; most assuredly it shall not get me wholly down." . . . With awe . . . one reads the consequence. One biographer, himself a musician, puts it thus: "We are eternal debtors to his deafness. It is doubtful if such lofty music could have been created except as self-compensation for some such affliction, and in the utter isolation which that affliction brought about." So Beethoven made all things work together for good. . . .

When life puts something up to us we need not *react*; we can *respond*. That is different. That takes our spiritual contribution in. . . .

In our capacity to make that spiritual response to life our freedom lies.

—Harry Emerson Fosdick

I thought I would feel cut off by my illness from the rest of the human world. Instead, I found that human contacts grow warm, they glow, when you are in trouble. Family loyalties strengthen. The bonds grow firmer with friends and neighbors, and we become one family. Distant friends somehow learn what has happened; you hear from boyhood chums with whom you had lost all contact. The grandsons who come to visit on the lawn outside the hospital window—how additionally precious are their unseamed faces, their clear voices, their handsome soundness of feature and limb! . . .

A few days after the operation the March on Washington took place. I asked to have the television set connected and watched all day. For me the great moment came when Marian Anderson, in that universal voice which so incredibly combines the earthly with the heavenly, sang, "He's got the whole world in his hands." The words, so nobly simple, expressed the whole drama of what I had been feeling. I do not cry easily, but tears blurred the image of that humbly expressive face on the screen—tears not of sorrow or even of thanksgiving, but of a sense of the fullness of life and its oneness.

—Bradford Smith

APPROACHING THE UNKNOWN

To move from blindness to sight, from shutness to openness, from bondage to freedom—that is our journey and our destiny.

—E. Graham Howe and L. Le Mesurier

THE WIDEST HORIZON

Sooner or later, whatever our occupation, we sense the mystery of existence and the quest for a deeper meaning begins. When eyesight changes in middle life, often requiring glasses, the inner focus changes too. Searching for reality that includes but is not limited to the outer world, we begin to see further into life's meaning. Those who discover their basic spiritual nature and begin to relate to others at that level find their horizon widening in proportion to their depth of understanding and concern. Growth of this sort becomes a lifelong adventure.

The last half of life certainly requires more adjustments than the first half if we are to achieve acceptance of trials and serenity. But for those who have sensed that they are more than body and intellect, who have become convinced that their being is related to a Divine Purpose that can use every human experience of suffering to enlighten, bless, and transform their lives, these later years can be as satisfying as any before.

In a less active period, we can take time to recall and give thanks for blessings, for "every good and perfect gift" life has bestowed that heretofore we've taken for granted. We can use a daily quiet hour to pray for those we love, for friends in difficulty, and for the solution of world problems that only God can solve.

If we desire peace of mind we must rid ourselves of all resentments lodged below the level of conscious thought. Even if you feel you have been wronged without justification, that festering abscess must be brought to the surface and consigned to God. Pray that every hidden sore be uncovered, and as they are revealed, ask that they be cast out and replaced with God's healing peace. Before that can take place, you must admit your sin (resentment) and ask forgiveness. Doing so opens the way for his will to be done in that other life as well as in your own. That way lies peace.

When I was young, I used to wonder how I could possibly "love" unlovable people. In time I came to realize that such people are "unlovable" because they have too little love in themselves to nourish their own natures, let alone give any away. They are like the Beast in the fairy tale, abhorred for his ugliness till Beauty, out of tender compassion, kissed him—and by that act transformed him into a prince. Though we do not know the causes of their affliction we can offer compassion without words; we can pray that God will meet their deepest needs, and so transform them. Today, knowing that I too have failed him many times, I ask forgiveness for those sins he calls to mind and pray, "Change what needs to be changed, Holy Spirit. Let me become a channel of your love. Let your purpose be fulfilled in my life!"

In my thirties I expected the later years to be a downhill plodding: at best a courageous endurance of limitations I would chafe against, at worst a tiresome wait for release from increasing physical handicaps. Instead, it has been filled with abundance of joys. Relationships have mellowed. I have been given friends who "speak the same language," whose lives mesh with mine at a deeper level than most. Creativity has increased. Years of collecting "food for the spirit" from worldwide sources have borne rich fruitage in helping others bear deep sorrow and surmount their troubles. Every day brings new occasions for thanksgiving—free gifts of love from the Source of Being whom I asked to take charge of my life so long ago.

If you are still walking alone, finding the way dreary and dreading what lies ahead, turn now and in your own way and words say, "Come, dear God; I need you—I need your strength. Be my guide; I want your purpose for me to be fulfilled."

Perhaps you have been resisting such a daring step thus far because of disturbing doubts: "What if he changed me so I wouldn't be myself?" "What if he turned me into a saint? I don't want to be a saint." "What if surrendering self made me fanatical or strange?"

I understand perfectly, having delayed for those very reasons myself. What happened when I finally capitulated was that all sorts of petty fears dropped away. I ceased to feel fragmented and became "every whit whole." I also found a simple way to judge what are God's assignments and what are not, so at this stage of development I feel no guilt even about refusing requests for service in "good causes."

Paul Tillich has called this transformation in a human being "the New Reality." If you decide to embrace this New Reality, if you let it grasp you and follow where the Holy Spirit abiding in you leads, the years ahead will bring you a fulfillment nothing can prevent.

And if you are "eternally important, eternally loved," you have nothing to fear, even at the approach of death. You will merely step out of an earthly habitation that has become a burden. For me, death is only an incident, a swift transfer from this plane of consciousness to a higher, where my deathless spirit will be set free for further learning and fresh adventures.

May the pages that follow bring you the same assurance. May trustful surrender bring you the same strength in times of weakness and triumph in days of trouble and dispel all fear of the unknown. Beyond the widest horizon that we face New Life awaits.

Dorothy Mason Fuller

Many people never climb above the plateau of forty-to-fifty. The signs that presage growth, so similar, it seems to me, to those of early adolescence—discontent, restlessness, doubt, despair, longing—are interpreted falsely as signs of decay. In youth one does not as often misinterpret the signs; one accepts them, quite rightly, as growing pains. One takes them seriously, listens to them, follows where they lead. One is afraid. Naturally. Who is not afraid of pure space—that breathtaking empty space of an open door? But despite fear, one goes through to the room beyond.

But in middle age, because of the false assumption that it is a period of decline, one interprets these life-signs paradoxically, as signs of approaching death. Instead of facing them, one runs away; one escapes—into depressions, nervous breakdowns, drink, love affairs, or frantic, thoughtless overwork. . . . Anything, rather than stand still and learn from them. One tries to cure the signs of growth, to exorcise them, as if they were devils, when really they might be angels of annunciation.

Angels of annunciation of what? Of a new stage of living when, having shed many of the physical struggles, the worldly ambitions, the material encumbrances of active life, one might be free to fulfill the neglected side of one's self. One might be free for growth of mind, heart, and talent; free at last for spiritual growth.

—*Anne Morrow Lindbergh*

The pessimist resembles a man who observes with fear and sadness that his wall calendar, from which he daily tears a sheet, grows thinner with each passing day. On the other hand, the person who attacks the problems of life actively is like a man who removes each successive leaf from his calendar and files it neatly and carefully away with its predecessors, after first having jotted down a few diary notes on the back. He can reflect with pride and joy on all the richness set down in these notes, on all the life he has aready lived to the full. What will it matter to him . . . that he is growing old? . . . What reasons has he to envy a young person? For the possibilities that a young person has, the future that is in store for him? "No, thank you," he will think. "Instead of possibilities, I have realities in my past, not only the reality of work done and of love loved, but of suffering suffered. These are the things of which I am most proud, though these are things which cannot inspire envy."

—Dr. Viktor E. Frankl

All who have meant good work with their whole hearts, have done good work, although they may die before they have time to sign it. Every heart that has beat strong and cheerfully has left a hopeful impulse behind it in the world, and bettered the tradition of mankind.

—Robert Louis Stevenson

There is a saying that he who would make a success of old age must start young. It may also be said that he who would make a success of dying must do it in the life he is living. Doctors and ministers know that the manner of a person's death is often in keeping with his life. . . .

Whether our time on earth is of long or short duration is not nearly so important as the quality of our living, the service we give in our different ways, the love we set in motion. When the moment comes and the secret call is heard, however it reaches the inner ear, the one who has been living fully and zestfully in the present will no doubt discover that he is quite ready for another kind of present. Now, the reach has at last outdistanced the grasp. When the habitation of the body is needed no longer, I think it is as willingly relinquished as the bird relinquishes the shell that gave it safe lodging until it was ready to break through it.

When John Quincy Adams, at the age of eighty, was asked one day how he was feeling, he replied, "I thank you, John Quincy Adams is well, sir, quite well. But the house in which he lives at present is becoming dilapidated. . . . The old tenement is becoming almost uninhabitable, and I think John Quincy Adams will have to move out of it very soon; but he himself, sir, is quite well, sir, quite well."

—Elizabeth Yates

"I am still learning." Michelangelo took these words as his motto right up to the end of his long life. This great painter, sculptor and poet died on the threshold of his 90th year, while working on vast architectural tasks and responsibilities, still filled with the same fierce desire of perfection he had shown in his younger years. . . .

There are many ways of learning and growing, and in each of us lie unplumbed depths waiting for development. In the autumn of our lives most of us—at last—have time on our hands and at the "turning of the tide" we are given the chance of a lifetime to begin anew, each according to his nature. What to do with that time, whether we waste it or use it, whether we enjoy it or let it depress us, depends on ourselves alone. . . .

Life's perspective expands as one grows older. Instead of blocking the view with a large self in the foreground, one sees, perhaps for the first time, other people, other things, in the radiance of a new objective light, undisturbed by that shadow of self. . . .

Most of life is a rush and a scramble and it is rare that we have time, except when we are growing old. Then everything, but *everything* can be turned into a joy or interest, even pain, as we are given more and more of that precious gift of leisure to think, "to see life clearly and to see it whole."

—*Barbara Greene*

What are the qualities we associate with old age more than any other time of life? What are the outer signs of the person one hopes to be after middle age has been left behind?

The first quality . . . is dignity, which definitely is not an attribute of youth. It betokens self-respect coupled with respect for others, as contrasted with the heedlessness of the young and of older persons who have not matured when and as they should.

Graciousness, like dignity, is acquired with the passing of the years, and neither can be assumed successfully, for both are spontaneous outgrowths of self-discipline. Graciousness is kindness expertly expressed.

Dignity and graciousness are admirable attributes, but wisdom is the most prized possession of the aged: to them it is what a fine physique is to youth—power.

Patience is wisdom's friend and ally, whose gift to their association is serenity. Accompanied by patience, wisdom finds new fields of usefulness as well as wider opportunities for growth.

Dignity, graciousness, patience, serenity, and wisdom mature slowly under experience's steady rays and, like many other fruits of mind and heart and spirit, they do not reach perfection until "the last of life for which the first was made."

—E. B. Prouty

Let us see to it that our lives, like jewels of great price, be noteworthy not because of their width but because of their weight. Let us measure them by their performance, not by their duration. We should therefore praise and number in the company of the blest that man who has invested well the portion of time, however little, that has been allotted to him; for such a one has seen the true light. He has not only lived but flourished. . . . Why do you ask: "How long did he live?" He still lives. At one bound he has passed over into posterity and has consigned himself to the guardianship of memory. . . .

And what, you ask, is the full span of life? It is living until you attain wisdom. He who has attained wisdom has reached, not the furthermost, but the most important goal. Such a one may indeed exult boldly and give thanks to the gods and count himself nature's creditor for having lived. He will indeed have the right to do so, for he has paid her back a better life than he received.

—*Seneca*

All vital relationships are in the process of change, of growth, and must perpetually be building themselves new forms. Those who try to live in some past only, whose sole ties to reality are the experiences they had in days gone by, miss life's deepest joy—to keep alive today, to grow now and all our days to the end.

—Ralph N. Helverson

Man first puts on the grosser things of nature, his body is from them; but by death he puts these off, and retains the purer things of nature which are nearest to spiritual things; and these then are his continents.

—Emmanuel Swedenborg

A long life makes me feel nearer truth, yet it won't go into words. . . . I want to tell people approaching and perhaps fearing old age that it is a time of discovery. If they say—"Of what?" I can only answer, "We must find out for ourselves, otherwise it won't be discovery." I want to say—"If at the end of your life you have only yourself, it is much. Look, you will find."

—Florida Scott-Maxwell

As I grow older, I grow calm. . . . I do not lose my hopes. . . . I think it possible that civilization will last as long as I care to look ahead—perhaps with smaller numbers, but perhaps also bred to splendor and greatness by science. I think it not improbable that man, like the grub that prepares a chamber for the winged thing it never has seen but is to be—that man may have cosmic destinies he does not understand. And so beyond the vision of battling races and an impoverished earth, I catch a dreaming glimpse of peace.

—Justice Oliver Wendell Holmes

As we grow older we become certain of this—that as the curve of our physical vitality dips, the curve of our essential personality ascends. Less and less can a man express himself in terms of his body, but there is more of him to express if only he could. That is why it is so hard to grow old gracefully and to accept the cramping limitation. But for some men that limitation was always there. How many of our greatest writers, painters, musicians have been invalids, a few of them painful and grotesque even to look at, but a mighty spirit was in them, as all the generations have known.

—W. H. Elliott

Age does not hope much for itself. It has attained the things youth hoped for, or it has found out their fallacy. But it keeps up, when it is an age of noble dwelling in God, hope for man and steadfast faith in man's high destiny. . . .

Faith and hope have been changed within the old man into new powers of love. Love . . . is his very life, the sunshine in which he waits for death. This inner life of love passes outwards into all who touch him, and is like a summer atmosphere in which they are warmed and made happier; in which men's sorrows and pains are healed and mercy poured on wrong, and sins covered, and quarrels atoned, and injuries forgotten. An exquisite gentleness, a mellowed justice, an inexhaustible forgiveness, ought to be the old man's heritage. . . .

It is now . . . that all the best things are in flower; love, mercy, righteousness, joy, peace, sympathy with man; and the more perfect they are, the more they carry with them conviction of their immortality.

—Stopford A. Brooke

Many of us have all our lives battened on praise, and only given of our best when we were warmed by approval and adulation. Take away all such props . . . and what will be left? All our facade means nothing to God, for the true self exists only as far as, denying its "I," it makes room for God's indwelling. He in His wonderful mercy provides this blessed time of age to scrape away the false fronts, to leave us as we truly are, giving us, if we ask, the grace to know ourselves and stretch our wills to his work, which, now unimpeded by our egotisms, He can do in us. . . . You must never say, "I am all alone in the world," but rather "God and I are alone"; and as you open your heart more and more to Him . . . you are able to be filled with His love which flows through you to embrace all men. Slowly it works but surely, so that there comes a time when no person is any longer distasteful to you, none misunderstood, none a nuisance. Your love desires great goodness for them all and, as you become a deep well of charity which shuts out no one, it ministers unseen to an unknown multitude.

—Sibyl Harton

So long as we love, we serve; so long as we are loved by others, I should say that we are almost indispensable, and no man is useless while he has a friend.

—Robert Louis Stevenson

Is it not possible that by living our lives we create something fit to add to the store from which we came? Our whole duty may be to clarify and increase what we are, to make our consciousness a finer quality. The effort of one's entire life would be needed if we are to return laden to our source.

We may well fear that we will bring too small a gift, that we garner little. But are we fit judges, and out of travail and ignorance and loss, may we not create a kernel of gold that we dare not know, but which will be claimed?

I must ask myself, "What have I to become immortal? Not my beloved ego, none of that. And the spirit in us that is truly there, is that not already immortal?" Some rare people may have a special role to play, and they may remain themselves after death, but how worthy of immortality are most of us? We have to believe we have value, we could not have courage otherwise, and our sense of being more than ourselves is our most precious possession. It is in honour of this feeling that we endure and try. Even the most meagre life will have a wealth of patience, a treasure of endurance, immeasurable courage and cheer, and kindness culled from laborious days, and these are surely gifts worthy of return.

—Florida Scott-Maxwell

If you have eternity to live in, how can it matter that this little stretch, here in this world, is coming to an end? I picture old age rather as a rest before the next great adventure. You are launched forever: you cannot stop; but you are allowed to rest before your next great lesson. But to think that that holiday is the end, or that it does not matter how your holiday is spent, is senseless. If you really believe that you have an immortal spirit, up to the last moment of your life you should be learning; up to the last instant of your life you should be finding out something; up to the last breath you draw there should be some new experience—experience of work, of joy, of suffering, of sympathy, of fellowship, of rest.

—Dr. Agnes Maude Royden

Progress consists in an eternal seeking, a never-ending attempt to find ever new and richer meanings in life.

—James Jackson Putnam

Memories in old age are a dispensation of Providence, a great solace. To me, memories are the Bread of Life. Nature has mercifully provided that . . . the happy ones stand out in relief, whereas those that are less happy fade into the background. Solitude ceases to be a synonym for loneliness when we cultivate these memories of our living past, keep them with us at will. But blessed are they who go on making memories up to the end of their days.

—*John Knittel*

You may say, what about the real pain of growing old, which is the closeness of that dark shadow at the end of the road? Death. For those of no belief, death means simply a long sleep, something, after all, that is faced every night. And for those happier beings who have the gift of faith in God, surely they will remember the words of the Gospel and "become again as little children," for, as every doctor and every psychiatrist knows, little children have no fear of death. A lifetime of experience must surely have taught us enough to enable us to take the final step in peace and dignity. But until that moment comes, much still remains for us to discover, to learn and to enjoy. Let us, therefore, open our eyes and our hearts and *live*.

—*Barbara Greene*

In the last stage the noble soul does two things: first, she returns to God as to that haven whence she set forth when she came to enter on the sea of this life; secondly, she blesses the journey which she has finished, because it has been straight and good, and free from bitterness of storm. And as a good mariner when he draws near to the harbor lets down his sails, and enters it gently with slight headway on, so we ought to let down the sails of our worldly pursuits, and turn to God with all our understanding and heart, so that we may come to that haven with all composure and with all peace.

—Dante Alighieri

Whatever may be my fate, I should wish to return to God a grateful and enraptured soul.

—André Gide

I look forward to the great adventure with awe, but not with apprehension. I have always stood in the bow, with hopeful anticipation of the life before me. When I put out to sea, I think I shall be standing in the bow and looking forward with eager curiosity and glad hopefulness to the new world to which the unknown voyage will bring me.

—Lyman Abbott

Suppose that the nature of things should of a sudden lift up her voice, and . . . rebuke some of us: "Why is death so great a thing to thee, mortal, that thou dost give way overmuch to sickly lamentation? Why groan and weep at death? For if the life that is past and gone has been pleasant to thee, why dost thou not retire like a guest sated with the banquet of life, and with calm mind embrace . . . a rest that knows no care? But if all thou hast reaped hath been wasted and lost, why seek to add more; why not rather make an end of life and trouble? For there is naught more which I can devise or discover to please thee."

What answer can we make but that nature brings a just charge against us? . . .

The old ever gives place, thrust out by new things. There must needs be substance that the generations to come may grow. Life is granted to none for freehold, to all on lease.

—*Lucretius*

The life of man is by no means limited to its short passage through this world. Death is only an illusion which hides from us the continuing development of life. And, moreover, we are generally dead in many respects before the actual moment which completes our transformation. Interior changes gradually make us realize that, in spite of all our vicissitudes, we are indeed immortal, with a life, an endless activity, which death does not cut short: far from it.

Whatever time, therefore, we may have lost in this world through circumstances which have checked our activity, is a small matter compared to the life without end which dwells in us and which will easily catch us up later on. . . .

Life limited by death? Nonsense! That is a great mistake. Death hardly counts; it is a mere appearance; we already have eternal life and that reflection should give us great tranquillity. . . .

Do not therefore be afraid of death. It is the flowering of life, the consummation of union with God.

—Abbé de Tourville

Death is not extinguishing the light; it is putting out the lamp because the dawn has come.

—Rabindranath Tagore

God . . . knoweth what he doeth. Do thou fear and be good. For whatsoever way He will that thou depart hence, let Him find thee ready. For here thou art a sojourner, not a possessor of the house. For this house is let to thee, not given; loth though thou be, thou must depart from it; neither hast thou received it on such terms, as that thou hast any fixed time. What saith my Lord? "Whensoever I will, whensoever I shall say, Depart, be thou ready. I drive thee from thy lodging but I will give thee a home; thou art a sojourner on earth, thou shalt be possessor in Heaven."

—St. Augustine

All mankind is of one Author, and is one volume; when one man dies, one chapter is not torn out of the book, but translated into a better language; and every chapter must be so translated. God employs several translators; some pieces are translated by age, some by sickness, some by war, some by justice; but God's hand is in every translation, and His hand shall bind up all our scattered leaves again for that library where every book shall lie open to one another.

—John Donne

Death is homecoming. . . . We set sail upon an unknown sea, but we go not to a strange land. Here we are pilgrims and strangers; there we shall be at home. . . . All of us have sent some friends before us, a brother, a sister, a child, a husband, a wife. When we are summoned to our departure, though the ship be strange and the sea unknown, we shall be embarking for a land where friends will be awaiting us.

—Lyman Abbott

My life is ending, I know that well, but every day that is left me I feel how my earthly life is in touch with a new infinite, unknown, but approaching life, the nearness of which sets my heart quivering with rapture, my mind glowing and my heart weeping with joy.

—Fyodor Dostoevsky

The ascetics and the self-indulgent divide things into good and evil—as it were to throw away the evil:

But things cannot be divided into good and evil, but all are good as soon as they are brought into subjection.

And seest thou not that except for Death thou couldst never overcome Death—

For since by being a slave to things of sense thou hast clothed thyself with a body which thou art not master of, thou wert condemned to a living tomb were that body not to be destroyed.

But now through pain and suffering out of this tomb shalt thou come; and through the experience thou hast acquired shalt build thyself a new and better body;

And so on many times, till thou spreadest wings and hast all powers diabolic and angelic concentrated in thy flesh.

—Edward Carpenter

There are brave and fortunate deaths. In the case of a certain man I saw death cut the thread of a marvelously advancing progress, in the flower of its growth, with an end so lofty that, in my opinion, his ambitious and courageous designs contained nothing so high as was their interruption. He reached the place to which he aspired, without making his way to it, more grandly and gloriously than he could have hoped or desired. And he surpassed by his fall the power and name to which he aspired in his career.

In judging the life of another, I always observe how the end was borne; and one of the principal concerns of my own life is that the end be borne well, that is, calmly and insensibly.

—Montaigne

Notwithstanding all that I have suffered, notwithstanding all the pain and weariness and anxiety and sorrow that necessarily enter into life. . . I would end my record with thanksgiving to the great Author of my being. . . . I would have it to be gratitude for all that belongs to my life and being—for joy and sorrow, for health and sickness, for success and disappointment, for virtue and for temptation, for life and death; because I believe that all is meant for good.

—Orville Dewey

[In his memoirs, written in the third person, a noted doctor described his experience after being stricken with a fatal disease. An old medical friend had just confirmed his suspicions.]

In those few minutes . . . something took place in his mind that he regarded as a sort of compensatory adjustment to the thought that he would soon be dead. In the prospect of death, life seemed to be given new meaning and fresh poignancy. It seemed from that moment as though all that his heart felt and his senses perceived were taking on a "deep autumnal tone" and an increased vividness. From now on, instead of being saddened, he found—to his own delighted astonishment

—that his sensitiveness to the simplest experiences was infinitely enhanced. . . .

He felt a deeper tenderness for the people whom he loved, and a warmer sympathy and understanding for many whose friendship he had lost in one way or another. . . .

As his disease caught up with him, he felt increasingly grateful for the fact that death was coming to him with due warning and gradually . . . thankful that he had time to compose his spirit and to spend a last year in affectionate and actually merry association with those dear to him.

—Dr. Hans Zinsser

Being is greater than doing. . . . If day by day we say, "My God, I offer thee these last days of my life" believing there is a purpose in that act of giving, the quiet, sedentary inactivity will hold no fret or frustration but a serene, tranquil peace, precious in itself.

—Sibyl Harton

In sickness when we are hanging between life and death, and physicians are watching over us and noting the symptoms hour by hour, we can do nothing better than lie still and see the salvation of the Lord. Whether our prayer is "O spare me that I may recover strength," or "Into Thy hands I commit my spirit," we are ready to leave the event with God. It is our duty, if we can, to recover; and it is our best hope of recovery to be patient and to cast our burden upon the Lord.

—Benjamin Jowett

Do not be anxious about death even though you feel it to be imminent and have every reason for despair, but give yourself up all the more to the mercy of God. . . . Death is frightening only when it is far off, and it is useless to think of it from our present standpoint. I have seen many people die, and not one of them had the slightest fear of death when it was there.

—Abbé de Tourville

I acknowledge unto thee, O Lord, that both my cure and my death are in thy hands. If death be determined by thee, I will in love accept it at thy hand. Make known to me the path of life: in thy presence is fulness of joy. Into thy hand I commend my spirit. Amen and Amen.

—prayer for a sickbed

The shock of death has always made love appear a greater thing than we knew before the baffling crisis came upon us. It has, too, by the same shock of contrast, awakened man to the full comprehension of the moral sublimity of the good life. Kant maintained that the sense of the sublime is due to the fact that when we are confronted with the supreme powers of nature we then become aware of something unfathomable in ourselves, and feel that we are superior to the might of the storm, or the mountain or the cataract. Nowhere is this truer than when man—man in his full, rich powers—is confronted by death. Instead of cringing in fear, he rises to an unaccustomed height of greatness and is utterly superior to death and aware of some quality in himself which death cannot touch. It is just then in that moment of seeming disaster and dissolution that a brave, good man is most triumphant and ready to burn all bridges behind him in his great adventure.

—Rufus Jones

"So death will come to fetch you?"

"No, not death but God Himself. . . . The catechism teaches that death is the separation of the soul from the body, that is all. I am not afraid of a separation which will unite me forever with God."

—St. Thérèse of Lizieux

[A heroic man's farewell to his wife written April 4, 1943, with manacled hands in a Nazi prison.]

In another five hours I shall be executed.

A great peace fills me, and a feeling of great lightness. All that is heavy has fallen away. And never have I possessed your love and the love of others so purely, so deeply, and so unflawed. I am happy in an inexplicable fashion. Keep me thus in memory. . . .

In a high pale blue spring sky there floated a small white cloud. A few breaths later, it had dissolved in the all. Did it therefore exist any less than before? Nothing that once has been can pass away. The face of the world retains it.

A deep, liberating peace encircles me. An astounding emotion wells up in me and fills me wholly: the essential element in life and in man is not affected by death. And so I remain completely with you, and you with me. I die with an exaltation that does not tolerate even tears. I stand face to face with the world in inexpressible purity, stand at its center, and these last hours are in truth the zenith of life—the zenith of life.

—Alfred Schmidt-Sas

Socrates feared nothing and death least of all. He compared man's way of meeting destiny with that of the trumpeting swan. "Will you not allow that I have as much of the spirit of prophecy in me as the swans?" he asked his friend Simmias. "For they, when they perceive that they must die, having sung all their life long, do then sing more lustily than ever, rejoicing in the thought that they are about to go away to the God whose ministers they are. But men, because they are themselves afraid of death, slanderously affirm of the swans that they sing a lament at the last, not considering that no bird sings when cold, or hungry, or in pain.

. . . I would not go out of life less merrily than the swans."

—C. L. Sulzberger

All men had within them a guide, a spark of the true light which could lead them to the full light of truth. This was Socrates' basic belief, in the words of the Gospel of St. John, "the true light which lighteth every man that cometh into the world." His own mission, he believed, was to open blind eyes, to make men realize the darkness of their ignorance and evil and so to arouse in them a longing for the light; to induce them to seek until they caught a glimpse of the eternal truth and goodness "without variableness or shadow of turning" which underlay life's confusions and futilities. . . .

It was the one concern of his life that they should find it. They were so made that only then . . . could they really live, fulfilling at last their own nature, in harmony with reality, with God. . . .

He proved the truth of what he said by his life and even more by his death. He showed men what they could become, their own spiritual possibilities, and showed them how they could meet "the mighty stranger, death."

When he was arrested and taken to court, he . . . refused to save his life by promising to give up teaching, but he did so with complete courtesy. . . .

"Strange, indeed, would my conduct be, O men of

Athens, if I who (on the battlefield) remained where the generals placed me, facing death like any other man, if now when God orders me, I were to desert through fear of death. Men of Athens, I honour and love you, but I shall obey God rather than you. . . . To you and to God I commit my cause, to be determined by you as is best for you and for me."

When the sentence of death had been pronounced he ended his reply . . . to the judges, "Be of good cheer . . . and know for a certainty that no evil can happen to a good man either in life or after death. I see clearly . . . the time has come for me to die . . . so my accusers have done me no harm. Still—they did not mean to do me good, and for this I may gently blame them. And now we go our ways, you to live and I to die. Which is better only God knows."

—Edith Hamilton

I have got my leave. Bid me farewell, my brothers! I bow to you all and take departure.

Here I give back the keys of my door—and I give up all claims to my house. I only ask for last kind words from you.

We were neighbors for long, but I received more than I could give. Now the day has dawned and the lamp that lit my dark corner is out. A summons has come and I am ready for my journey.

—Rabindranath Tagore

[A man who suffered heart arrest in his car at a stoplight on a busy highway recalls what death was like in the twenty-three minutes when, to doctors, every sign of life was absent. Hospitalized, electric shocks revived his heartbeat.]

Dr. Roth later related: "I came to see you in the Coronary Care Unit. You were perfectly conscious. I asked how you felt, and your response was: 'I feel like I've been there and come back.' It was true: you were there and now you were back."

A hard time followed. I could not connect with the world around me. Was I really here now, or was it an illusion? Was that other condition of being I had just experienced the reality, or was that the illusion? I would lie there and observe my body with suspicion and amazement. It seemed to be doing things of its own volition and I was a visitor within. . . .

During those first few days I was two people. My absent-mindedness and strange detachment gave the doctors pause. Perhaps the brain had been damaged after all. . . .

On the sixth day there was a sudden change. When I woke up, the world around me no longer seemed so peculiar. Something in me had decided to complete the return trip. From that day on, recovery was rapid. Eight days later I was discharged from the hospital.

Now family, friends, and strangers began to ask "what death was like." Could I remember what had happened during those twenty-three minutes when heart and breathing stopped? I found that experience could not easily be communicated.

Later, feeling and thinking my way back into the experience, I discovered why I could not make it a simple recital of events: when I left my body I also left all sensory human tools behind with which we perceive the world we take for real. But I found that I now knew certain things about my place in our world and my relationship to that other reality. My knowing was not through my brain but with another part of me which I cannot explain.

For me, the moment of transition from life to death —what else can one call it?—was easy. There was no time for fear, pain or thought. There was no chance "to see my whole life before me" as others have related. The last impression I can recall lasted a brief instant. I was moving at high speed toward a net of great luminosity. The strands and knots where the luminous lines intersected were vibrating with a tremendous cold energy. The grid appeared as a barrier that would prevent further travel. I did not want to move through the grid. For a brief moment my speed appeared to slow down. Then I was in the grid. The instant I made contact with it, the vibrant luminosity increased to a blinding intensity which drained, absorbed and transformed me at the same time. There was no pain. The sensation was neither pleasant nor unpleasant but completely consuming. The nature of everything had changed. Words only vaguely approximate the experience from this instant on.

The grid was like a transformer, an energy converter transporting me through form and into formlessness, beyond time and space. Now I was not in a place, nor even in a dimension, but rather in a condition of being. This new "I" was not the I which I knew, but rather a distilled essence of it, yet something vaguely familiar, something I had always known buried under a superstructure of personal fears, hopes, wants and needs. This "I" had no connection to ego. It was final, unchangeable, indivisible, indestructible pure spirit. While completely unique and individual as a fingerprint, "I" was, at the same time, part of some infinite, harmonious and ordered whole. I had been there before.

The condition "I" was in was pervaded by a sense of great stillness and deep quiet. Yet there was also a sense of something momentous about to be revealed, a further change. But there is nothing further to tell except of my sudden return to the operating table.

I would like to repeat that these experiences outside the dimensions of our known reality did not "happen" as if I were on some sort of a voyage I could recollect. Rather, I discovered them afterward, rooted in my consciousness as a kind of unquestionable knowing. . . . A recurrent nostalgia remains for that other reality, that condition of indescribable stillness and quiet where the

"I" is the part of a harmonious whole. The memory softens the old drives for possession, approval and success. . . .

I am glad I am here and now. But I know that this marvelous place of sun and wind, flowers, children and lovers, this murderous place of evil, ugliness and pain, is only one of many realities through which I must travel to distant and unknown destinations. For the time being I belong to the world and it belongs to me.

—Victor D. Solow

One dearer to me than all else in life had, for days, lain helpless, speechless. Consciousness was gone. We knew that . . . the irremediable river must soon be crossed. The last morning of our watching was misty; the day emerged so wanly that we hardly knew that it had come. Suddenly the one we loved so dearly sat up in bed, a strange light on her face of a happiness past all our mortal joy. She stretched abroad her arms, crying in the radiant abandon of spiritual certainty, "The Dawn! The beautiful Dawn!"

Those were her dying words—glad, triumphant. And for me they hold the eternal promise of the sunrise. They glow with immortality. In every sense, our mortal dawn that day was anything but beautiful; but she saw the beginning of an immortal day. Believing in a God of infinite love and of infinite power, I find it natural to believe that death is not a disastrous sundown but rather a spiritual sunrise, ushering in the unconjectured splendors of immortality.

—Archibald Rutledge

Believe, my heart,
nothing is lost to you.
All is yours, yes,
all that you have loved
and striven for.

Believe, you were not
born in vain!
You have not lived
and suffered in vain!

What was born
must depart.

What has gone
shall rise again.
Be not fearful,
Prepare to live.

—Gustav Mahler

SOURCES

Page

1 Clifford Bax (English; 1886–1962), "Turn back, O man," stanza 2.

7 Glenn T. Seaborg, *Creative Suffering* (Kansas City, Mo.: National Catholic Reporter Publishing Co., 1970), pp. 57, 58. Used by permission of the National Catholic Reporter.

7 Alfred Noyes (English; 1880–1958), *The Edge of the Abyss*, The Josiah Wood Lectures for 1941 (Sackville, N.B., Canada: Mount Allison University, 1942), p. 4.

9 Martin Buber (German; 1878–1965), *To Hallow This Life* (New York: Harper, 1958), pp. 119–20. Copyright by Jacob Trapp, 1958. Used by permission of Harper & Row.

10 Harry Emerson Fosdick (1878–1969), *A Faith for Tough Times* (New York: Harper, 1952), pp. 14, 15, 16. Used by permission of Harper & Row.

11 Thomas Kelly (1893–1941), *A Testament of Devotion* (New York: Harper & Bros., 1941), pp. 114–15. Used by permission of Harper & Row.

12 Elizabeth O'Connor, *Our Many Selves* (New York: Harper & Row, 1971), p. 102. Used by permission of the publisher.

13 Franz E. Winkler, *Man: The Bridge between Two Worlds* (New York: Harper & Bros., 1960), pp. 48–49, 50. Used by permission of Harper & Row.

14 Wyatt Cooper, "Does Everybody Want To Be Somebody?" in *Harper's Bazaar*, May 1971. Reprinted by permission of Mr. Cooper.

Page

15 Antoine de Saint-Exupèry (French; 1900–1944), *Wind, Sand and Stars* (New York: Reynal & Hitchcock, 1939), pp. 47–48. Reprinted by permission of Harcourt, Brace Jovanovich, Inc.

16 Samuel Miller (1900–1968), *The Life of the Soul* (New York: Harper, 1951), pp. 34–35. Used by permission of Myra Miller Bryan and Word Books, 4800 West Waco Drive, Waco, Texas 76703.

17 Yehudi Menuhin, *Theme and Variations* (Briarcliff Manor, N.Y.: Stein & Day, 1972), p. 146. Copyright © 1972 by Yehudi Menuhin. Used by permission of Stein and Day Publishers and Heinemann Educational Books Ltd.

17 Erich Fromm, *The Revolution of Hope* (New York: Harper & Row, 1968), p. 141. Used by permission of the publisher.

18 A tribute from a company President personally known to me. Permission to use this material anonymously was given by an official of the company.

19 Georgia Harkness, *Prayer and the Common Life* (Nashville, Tenn.: Abingdon Press, 1948), p. 59. Copyright 1948 by Stone and Pierce (Abingdon Press). Used by permission of the publisher.

19 François de la Mothe Fénelon (French; 1651–1715).

20 Kelly, *A Testament of Devotion*, p. 116. Used by permission.

21 Michel Quoist (French), *The Meaning of Success*, trans. Donald P. Gray (Notre Dame, Ind.: Fides Publishers, 1963), p. 92. Reprinted with permission.

22 Alexis Carrel, M.D. (1873–1944), "Prayer Is Power," *The Reader's Digest*, March 1941. Copyright 1941 by The Reader's Digest Assn., Inc. Used by permission.

22 Rufus Jones (1863–1948), *A Call to What Is Vital* (New York: Macmillan, 1948), pp. 141–42. Copyright © 1948, reprinted by permission of the Macmillan Publishing Co., Inc.

Page

23 W. E. Channing (1780–1842), quoted in *Daily Strength for Daily Needs*, ed. Mary Tileston (New York: Grosset & Dunlap, 1884), p. 163.

23 Harkness, *Prayer and the Common Life*, pp. 28–29. Used by permission.

23 Sören Kierkegaard (Danish; 1813–1855).

24 Robert Leighton, Archbishop of Glasgow (English; 1611–1684).

24 Proverbs 3:5, 6, King James Version.

24 Elizabeth Gray Vining, *The World in Tune* (New York: Harper, 1954), p. 113. Used by permission of Pendle Hill Publications and the author.

25 John B. Coburn, *Prayer and Personal Religion* (Philadelphia: Westminster Press, 1957), pp. 18, 19, 20, 21. Copyright 1957 by W. L. Jenkins. Used with permission of the publisher.

26 Olive Wyon (English), *The School of Prayer*, 10th ed. (London: S.C.M. Press, 1962), p. 121. Copyright © 1943, used by permission of S.C.M. Press, Ltd. Copyright © 1963, reprinted by permission of the Macmillan Publishing Co., Inc.

26 Agnes Maude Royden (English; 1876–1956), *Consider the Days*, comp. Daisy Dobson (New York: Woman's Press, 1942), p. 7. Reprinted with permission of the National Board, Young Women's Christian Association of the USA.

26 Proverbs 8:17, King James Version.

27 Frederick Buechner, *The Magnificent Defeat* (New York: Seabury Press, 1966), p. 143. Used by permission of the publisher.

27 W. F. Adams, S.S.J.E., and Gilbert Shaw (English), *Triumphant in Suffering* (New York: Morehouse Gorham; London: A. R. Mowbray & Co., 1951), p. 39.

28 Wyon, *The School of Prayer*, p. 114. Used by permission.

29 Louis Evely (French), *That Man Is You*, trans. Edmond

Bonin (New York: Paulist Press, 1964), p. 128. Used by permission of the publisher.

29 Rufus Jones, in a magazine article.

31 Dame Julian of Norwich (English; 1343–1413).

36 Henry Scott Holland, Canon of St. Paul's, London (English; 1847–1918).

36 Dag Hammarskjöld (Danish; 1905–1961), *Markings*, trans. Leif Sjoberg and W. H. Auden (New York: Alfred A. Knopf, 1964), p. 8. Copyright © 1964 by Alfred A. Knopf, Inc. and Faber and Faber, Ltd., and reprinted by their permission.

37 John Howard Griffin, *Creative Suffering* (Kansas City, Mo.: National Catholic Reporter Publishing Co., 1970), pp. 28, 29, 30. Used by permission of the National Catholic Reporter.

38 Baron Friedrich von Hügel (German; 1852–1925), *Selected Letters*, ed. Bernard Holland (London and Toronto: J. M. Dent & Sons; New York: E. P. Dutton & Co., 1928), pp. 228, 230. Quoted in Douglas Steere, *Doors into Life* (New York: Harper, 1948), pp. 177–78. Used by permission of Harper & Row.

39 Louis Evely (French), *Suffering* (New York: Herder & Herder, 1967), p. 142. Copyright 1967 by Herder and Herder, Inc. Used by permission of the Seabury Press.

40 Edmond Holt Babbitt, *Pastor's Pocket Manual for Hospital and Sickroom* (Nashville, Tenn.: Abingdon Press, 1949), p. 82. Copyright 1949 by Pierce and Smith (Abingdon Press). Used by permission.

40 Brother Lawrence (Nicholas Herman of Lorraine; 1611–1691), *The Practice of the Presence of God* (New York: Fleming H. Revell Co., 1895), p. 55.

41 Douglas Steere (1901–1974), *Prayer in the Contemporary World* (New York: National Council of Churches of Christ in the USA, 1966), p. 10. Used with permission of Church Women United.

42 Evely, *Suffering*, p. 93. Used by permission.

Page

42 Babbitt, *Pastor's Pocket Manual for Hospital and Sickroom*, p. 86. Used by permission.

42 Horace (Roman; 65–8 B.C.).

43 John Patrick, *The Teahouse of the August Moon* (New York: G. P. Putnam's Sons, 1952), act I, scene 1. Copyright © 1952 by John Patrick.

43 Griffin, *Creative Suffering*, p. 34. Used by permission.

43 Marcus Aurelius (Roman; 121–180) *Meditations* 5. 18.

43 Samuel Johnson (English; 1709–1784).

44 W. H. Elliott (English), *My Scallop Shell* (London: A. R. Mowbray & Co.; New York: Morehouse Gorham, 1946), p. 114. Used by permission of A. R. Mowbray & Co.

44 Charles H. Brent (1862–1929), *Things That Matter*, ed. Frederick Kate (New York: Harper, 1945), p. 46. Used by permission of Harper & Row.

45 Viktor E. Frankl (Austrian), *Man's Search for Meaning* (Boston: Beacon Press, 1962), pp. 66, 67. Copyright © 1959, 1962 by Viktor Frankl. Reprinted by permission of Beacon Press and Hodder and Stoughton, Ltd.

46 François de la Mothe Fénelon (French; 1651–1715).

46 Plotinus (Roman; 205–270).

46 Hammarskjöld, *Markings*, p. 56. Used by permission.

48 Paul Tournier (Swiss), *The Person Reborn*, trans. Edwin Hudson (New York: Harper & Row, 1966; London: S. C. M. Press, Heinemann, 1967), pp. 133, 134. Used by permission.

49 George A. Buttrick, *God, Pain and Evil* (Nashville, Tenn.: Abingdon Press, 1966), pp. 210, 211. Used by permission.

49 Frankl, *Man's Search for Meaning*, pp. 114, 115, 116. Used by permission.

50 Dietrich Bonhoeffer (German; 1906–1945), *Letters from Prison*, rev. ed. (London: S. C. M. Press, 1967), p. 206. Copyright © 1952, reprinted by permission of the Macmillan Publishing Co., Inc. and S. C. M. Press, Ltd.

Page

50 Rabindranath Tagore (East Indian; 1861–1941), *Sādhanā* (New York: Macmillan, 1913), pp. 63–64. Copyright renewed 1941 by Rabindranath Tagore. Used by permission of the Macmillan Publishing Co., Inc. and by permission of the Tagore Estate and Macmillan London and Basingstoke.

51 O'Connor, *Our Many Selves*, pp. 99, 100. Used by permission.

52 Bradford Smith (1909–1964), *Dear Gift of Life* (Wallingford, Pa.: Pendle Hill, 1965), no. 142, p. 5. Used by permission.

52 George Meredith (English; 1828–1909).

52 Albert Camus (French; 1913–1960), cited in *Contemporary Quotations*, comp. James B. Simpson (New York: Thomas Y. Crowell, 1964), p. 294, where the *Christian Science Monitor*, 6 January 1960, is given as source.

53 Nicholas Berdyaev (Russian; 1874–1948), *The Destiny of Man* (New York: Charles Scribner, 1937), pp. 118–19. Used by permission of Harper & Row and Geoffrey Bles, Ltd.

54 Sam Keen, *Apology for Wonder* (New York: Harper & Row, 1969), pp. 207–8. Used by permission.

54 W. R. Inge, Dean of St. Paul's, London (English; 1860–1954), *A Life of Devotion* (London: Longmans Green, 1924), p. 86. Used by permission of Longman Group, Ltd.

55 Lowell Russell Ditzen, *Personal Security Through Faith* (New York: Holt, 1954), p. 170. Reprinted by permission of Holt, Rinehart and Winston, Inc.

56 Brother Lawrence, *Practice of the Presence of God*, p. 56.

56 Josiah Royce (1855–1916).

56 Evely, *Suffering*, p. 153. Used by permission.

57 Eleanor Roosevelt (1884–1962), *You Learn by Living* (New York: Harper & Row, 1960), pp. 29–30. Used

by permission of Harper & Row and Nannine Joseph, Agent.

57 E. B. Prouty, *explorations* (Pasadena: Anderson & Ritchie, 1946), p. 70.

57 Jones, *A Call to What Is Vital*, pp. 62–63. Used by permission.

58 Psalm 31:9, 10, King James Version.

58 Psalm 46:1, King James Version.

58 Marcus Aurelius (Roman; 121–180) *Meditations* 7. 64; 8. 28; 7. 33.

59 Leigh Hunt (English; 1784–1859).

59 A. E. Gould and Vernon Symonds (English), *Into the Valley* (London: Peter Davies, 1964), p. 200. Reprinted by permission of Peter Davies, Ltd.

59 Attributed to Kahlil Gibran (Lebanese; 1883–1931). Source not verified.

60 Evely, *Suffering*, p. 70. Used by permission.

60 Adams and Shaw, *Triumphant in Suffering*, pp. 16, 17.

61 Flora Slosson Wuellner, *To Pray and to Grow* (Nashville, Tenn.: Abingdon Press, 1970), p. 86. Used by permission.

61 Psalm 55:22, King James Version.

61 Psalm 91:15, King James Version.

62 Coburn, *Prayer and Personal Religion*, p. 93. Used by permission.

62 Edith Hamilton (1867–1963), *Witness to the Truth* (New York: W. W. Norton & Co., 1957), p. 230. Used by permission of W. W. Norton and Co., Inc. Copyright © 1948, 1957 by W. W. Norton and Co., Inc.

62 François de Sales (French; 1567–1622).

63 Evely, *Suffering*, p. 149. Used by permission.

63 George Fox (English; 1624–1691).

64 Evelyn Underhill (English; 1875–1941), *The Fruits of the Spirit* (London: Longman Green, 1956), pp. 11, 12. Used by permission of Longman Group, Ltd.

Page

64 Isaiah 26:3, King James Version.

64 Luke 23:46, King James Version.

64 David Grayson (Ray Stannard Baker; 1870–1946), *Under My Elm* (Garden City, N.Y.: Doubleday, Doran & Co., 1942), pp. 223–24. Copyright 1942 by Doubleday & Co. Used by permission.

65 William Penn (1644–1718), *Some Fruits of Solitude,* in *Remember William Penn* (Philadelphia: Wm. Penn Tercentenary Publication, 1944), "Reflections and Maxims," p. 23.

65 Abbé de Tourville (French; 1842–1903), *Letters of Direction* (London: A. & C. Black, Ltd., Dacre Press, 1939); p. 100. Reprinted by permission of Adam and Charles Black, Ltd.

66 Royden, *Consider the Days,* p. 45. Used with permission.

66 Harry Emerson Fosdick (1878–1969), *Dear Mr. Brown* (New York: Harper & Row, 1961), p. 81. Used by permission.

67 Jones, *A Call to What Is Vital,* pp. 76–77. Used by permission.

67 Ian Fraser, Lord of Lonsdale (British), *Whereas I Was Blind* (London: Hodder & Stoughton, 1942), p. 38. Used by permission.

68 Gould and Symonds, *Into the Valley,* p. 200, app. H. Used by permission.

69 Harry Emerson Fosdick (1878–1969), *The Secret of Victorious Living* (New York: Harper & Row, Chapel Books, 1966), pp. 6, 7, 8. Used by permission.

70 Smith, *Dear Gift of Life,* pp. 6, 7. Used by permission.

71 E. Graham Howe and L. Le Mesurier (English), *The Open Way* (London: J. M. Watkins, 1958), p. 136.

77 Anne Morrow Lindbergh, *Gift from the Sea* (New York: Pantheon Books, 1955), pp. 87–88. Copyright © 1955 by Anne Morrow Lindbergh. Used by permission of Pantheon Books, a Division of Random House, and Chatto and Windus, Ltd.

Page

78 Frankl, *Man's Search for Meaning*, p. 123. Used by permission.

78 Robert Louis Stevenson (1850–1894), *Aes Triplex* (New York: Charles Scribner's Sons, 1901), p. 24.

79 Elizabeth Yates, *Up the Golden Stair* (New York: E. P. Dutton, 1966), p. 36. Copyright © 1966 by Elizabeth Yates McGreal. Reprinted by permission of E. P. Dutton and Co., Inc.

80 Eva and Barbara Green, *The Chance of a Lifetime* (Freeport, Me.: Bond Wheelwright, 1968), pp. v, vi. Reprinted by permission of the Bond Wheelwright Co.

81 Prouty, *explorations*, p. 165. Used by permission.

82 Seneca (Roman; 4 B.C.–A.D. 65) *Epistles* 93.

83 Ralph N. Helverson, *Impassioned Clay* (Cambridge, Mass., privately printed, 1964), p. 61. Used by permission of Mr. Helverson.

83 Emmanuel Swedenborg (Swedish; 1845–1912), *Divine Providence* (London: J. M. Dent & Sons; New York: E. P. Dutton & Co., 1934), p. 167.

83 Florida Scott-Maxwell, *The Measure of My Days* (New York: Alfred A. Knopf, Borzoi Books, 1968), p. 142. Copyright © 1968 by Florida Scott-Maxwell. Reprinted by permission of Alfred A. Knopf, Inc. and Mrs. Scott-Maxwell.

84 Oliver Wendell Holmes, Jr., "Law and the Court," speech at a dinner of the Harvard Law School Association of New York, 15 February 1913, published in *The Mind and Faith of Justice Holmes*, ed. Max Lerner (Boston: Little, Brown & Co., 1943), p. 391.

84 Elliot, *My Scallop Shell*, pp. 16–17. Used by permission.

85 Stopford A. Brooke (Irish; 1832–1916), *The Life Superlative* (Boston: Beacon Press, 1907), pp. 195–97.

86 Sibyl Harton, *On Growing Old* (London: Hodder and Stoughton; New York: Morehouse-Gorham, 1957), p. 82. Reprinted by permission of Hodder and Stoughton, Ltd. and Morehouse-Barlow.

Page

86 Robert Louis Stevenson (1850–1894), *Lay Morals and Other Papers* (New York: Charles Schribner's Sons, 1911), p. 50.

87 Scott-Maxwell, *The Measure of My Days*, pp. 40–41. Used by permission.

87 Attributed to Agnes Maude Royden in *Assurances of Life Eternal*, comp. Margaret E. Burton (New York: Thomas Y. Crowell, 1959), pp. 57–58.

87 James Jackson Putnam, as cited in Margaret Ames, *For Those New to Sorrow* (New York: privately printed, 1962), p. 77.

88 John Knittel, quoted in Greene, *The Chance of a Lifetime*, p. 125. Used by permission.

88 Greene, *The Chance of a Lifetime*, pp. vii-viii. Used by permission.

89 Dante Alighieri (Italian; 1265–1321).

95 André Gide (French; 1869–1951), *Travels in the Congo*, trans. Dorothy Bussy (Berkeley and Los Angeles: University of California Press, 1962), p. 17. Translation copyright 1929, 1957 by Alfred A. Knopf, Inc. Used by permission of Alfred A. Knopf, Inc.

89 Lyman Abbott (1835–1922), *Reminiscences* (Boston and New York: Houghton Mifflin Co., 1915), p. 493. Used by permission of Mrs. Robert W. Hellum.

90 Lucretius (Roman; 96–65 B.C.) *On the Nature of Things* 3. 931–71.

91 de Tourville, *Letters of Direction*, p. 109. Used by permision.

91 Rabindranath Tagore (East Indian; 1861–1941), as found in *Assurances of Life Eternal*, comp. Margaret Burton (New York: Thomas Y. Crowell, 1959), p. 42. See also Tagore, *Sādhanā*, p. 94, where the figure is expressed in somewhat different words.

91 St. Augustine (354–430).

92 John Donne (English; 1573–1631).

92 Lyman Abbott (1835–1922), *The Other Room* (New

York: Macmillan Co., 1904), pp. 117–19. Used by permission of Mrs. Robert W. Hellum.

92 Fyodor Dostoevsky (Russian; 1821–1881), *The Brothers Karamazov.*

93 Edward Carpenter (English; 1844–1929), *Towards Democracy* (London: Allen & Unwin, 1905), pt. 3, "The Secret of Time and Satan," pp. 362–63.

94 Michel de Montaigne (French; 1533–1592), essay entitled "Judge Not Happiness Till After Death," in *Selected Essays,* trans. Charles Cotton and W. Hazlitt, ed. Blanchard Bates (New York: Modern Library, 1949), pp. 12–13. Copyright 1949 by Random House, Inc.

94 Orville Dewey (1794–1882).

95 Hans Zinsser (1878–1940), *As I Remember Him* (Boston: Little, Brown & Co., 1940), chap. 26. Copyright 1939, 1940 by Hans Zinsser. Used by permission of Little, Brown & Co., in association with The Atlantic Monthly Press.

95 Harton, *On Growing Old,* p. 87. Used by permission.

96 Benamin Jowett (English; 1817-1893).

96 de Tourville, *Letters of Direction,* p. 109. Used by permission.

96 Source unknown.

97 Rufus Jones (1863–1948), *Spiritual Energies in Daily Life* (New York: Macmillan, 1922), pp. 123–25. Used by permission.

97 St. Thérèse of Lizieux (French; 1873–1897).

98 Alfred Schmidt-Sas (German), in *Dying We Live,* ed. Helmut Gollwitzer, Käthe Kuhn, and Reinhold Schneider, trans. Reinhard C. Kuhn (New York: Pantheon Books, 1956), pp. 177–78. Copyright © 1956 by Patheon Books Inc., reprinted by permission of Pantheon Books, Inc., a Division of Random House, Inc.

99 C. L. Sulzberger, *My Brother Death* (New York: Harper & Bros., 1961), pp. 9–10. Used by permission of Mr. Sulzberger.

Page

100 Hamilton, *Witness to the Truth*, pp. 33, 35, 36, 37. Used by permission.

100 Rabindranath Tagore (East Indian; 1861–1941), *Gitanjali* XCIII, from *Collected Poems and Plays of Rabindranath Tagore*, copyright 1913 by Macmillan Publishing Co., Inc., renewed 1941 by Rabindranath Tagore. Used by permission of the Macmillan Publishing Co., Inc. and by permission of the Tagore Estate and Macmillan London and Basingstoke.

104 Victor D. Solow, "I Died at 10:52 A.M.," *The Reader's Digest*, October 1974. Copyright 1974 by The Reader's Digest Assn., Inc. Used with permission.

105 Archibald Rutledge, *Peace in My Heart* (Garden City, N.Y.: Doubleday & Co., 1930), pp. 5–6. Used by permission.

105 Gustav Mahler (German; 1860–1911). Stanzas added by Mahler himself to the choral passages that end his Second Symphony. Translator unknown.

I wish to record here my deep appreciation of the invaluable services of Eleanor W. Hittinger, Elizabeth Stouffer, and Margaret Kaufmann in preparing the manuscript for publication.—D.M.F.